Getting

RENTAL
INCOME

The *Getting Started In* Series

Getting Started in

RENTAL INCOME

Michael C. Thomsett

WILEY

John Wiley & Sons, Inc.

Published by John Wiley & Sons, Inc., Hoboken, New Jersey
Published simultaneously in Canada

For general information on our other products and services or for technical support, please contact our Customer Care Department within the United States at (800) 762-2974, outside the United States at (317) 572-3993 or fax (317) 572-4002.

Wiley also publishes its books in a variety of electronic formats. Some content that appears in print may not be available in electronic books. For more information about Wiley products, visit our web site at www.wiley.com.

Library of Congress Cataloging-in-Publication Data:
Thomsett, Michael C.
  Getting started in rental income / Michael C. Thomsett.
     p. cm.
  Includes index.
  ISBN 0-471-71098-9 (pbk.)
  1. Real estate investment—Handbooks, manuals, etc. 2. Rental housing—Handbooks, manuals, etc. I. Title.
  HD1382.5.T5642 2005
  332.63'24--dc22

                                        2004030897
  ISBN-13 978-0-471-71098-1
  ISBN-10 0-471-71098-9

Printed in the United States of America

10 9 8 7 6 5 4 3 2 1

Contents

Chapter 4

Chapter 5

PART 2

Rental Income Investment Planning Strategies

Chapter 6

Getting Started in

RENTAL INCOME

A Market with Profit Potential

Buy a rental property, find a tenant, and collect rent. Is it really all that simple? Can you set up a situation in which your tenant pays your mortgage and you simply build equity over several years? Or is there more to it?

Of course, there is much more to creating rental income than the initial challenge. You have to come up with down payment money, get loan approval for your rental property, and judge the investment potential of the plan. You have to ensure that your income, plus cash flow from the rental, is going to be adequate to cover mortgage payments, taxes, insurance, and repairs—not to mention the occasional vacancy. There may be more risk than you are aware of as you start out, and before proceeding, it makes sense for you to study and understand those risks.

As with any new investment, knowledge is an essential and necessary starting point. If you have money in the stock market, you know that you cannot put all of your money into buying shares of stock without first investigating the company from several angles. The same is true in real estate. You have probably heard that "real estate values always go up," "demand increases every year," and "real estate is much safer than the stock market." These statements are partly true and may be true in context. Nevertheless, you have to consider that real estate values vary regionally and are based on such factors as the job market, vacancies, simple demand for housing, and price trends. Real estate values may always go up—but how long will it take to realize a profit from a real estate investment? That is the more important issue. The *timing* of your investment and the time you have to hold your rental property determine whether it is a worthwhile endeavor. Demand may increase every year, but where? It may be true

1

that demand is growing in your state or region, but not in your town. If employment is down, workers relocate. This means that many houses may be for sale and that there is no new construction. At the same time, there may be a real estate boom in a city only a few miles away, where employment rates are high and demand for housing is strong. Finally, it is true that real estate is safer than the stock market in some aspects. For example, you can insure real estate and you get special tax benefits other investments do not enjoy. Cash flow from rental income is attractive and can pay your mortgage for you. On the other hand, it is more difficult to move money around in real estate compared to the stock market. Your increment of investment in real estate is far higher and the market tends to move slowly. The stock market is higher-risk, but it is much more flexible.

Any comparison between real estate and other investments cannot be made with sweeping generalizations. Instead you need to understand the many aspects of risk and potential in order to understand real estate in context. The issues worth comparing include questions such as:

- How long do you need to hold onto a property before it will be profitable?
- How can you judge cash flow, and why is it so important?
- Can you make profits in flipping properties?
- Are you able to work on fixer-upper properties?
- What planning strategies do you have to do before you invest?
- What tax advantages will you have in real estate?
- How do you judge investment diversification with real estate?

These questions are at the core of any real estate investment program. Going beyond the rental income-specific question, you also need to view and judge real estate in the larger context of your long-term financial plan. For most families, that plan includes home ownership, savings, retirement plans, and equity investments (stocks and mutual funds). You may expand this long-term plan to include rental income, but to do this you also need to appreciate the specific risks and responsibilities that go with the rental income market. The profit potential is impressive; and it is true that a rent-paying tenant covers your mortgage payment. However, to summarize the entire real estate investment question by observing the positive aspects alone is self-deluding. An honest assessment of rental income reveals that while investment potential, cash flow, tax benefits, and profits are promising, all of those benefits have associated risks.

You should not be discouraged from pursuing the idea of including rental income in your portfolio. However, you are more likely to succeed in this endeavor if you study both potential risks along with rewards. This is true in the stock market, and it is equally true in real estate. This book is designed to address the important questions that should come up if you are thinking about buying real estate and generating rental income. There are many ways to gain both profits and satisfaction from this venture, including the sense of having personal, direct control over your investments. However, just as *location* is the central element to value in real estate, *knowledge* is the central element to investing success.

Part

Approaching the Market

The Traditional Approach

Buy, Hold, Hold a While Longer, Sell

The creation of rental income is not automatic. It does not come into existence simply by virtue of an investor buying rental property and finding a tenant. Successfully generating a long-term income stream from your rental income depends on advance research; an understanding of your local market—and a keen awareness of the many alternatives you face in terms of opportunity as well as risk.

In the stock market, the well-known buy–hold–sell implies the possibility of quick turnaround. The stock market itself can be a fast-paced experience. Day traders go in and out of positions, minute by minute, often making huge profits or suffering huge losses before lunch. Real estate investors cannot have the same experience. In real estate, the prices of properties do not change in the liquid environment of an auction marketplace like the stock market. The cost and time involved in completing real estate transactions requires a different mindset from that of the stock market. If you want to generate rental income, you need to appreciate the differences between stocks and real estate.

cash flow
the amount of cash moving in and out within an investment program. Cash flow has to be manageable in order to justify the investment, based on income, expenses, nondeductible payments, and tax benefits.

In this chapter, we learn about the differences between real estate and other investments, setting the stage for how the traditional approaches to markets work; how your investing, financial and personal life are affected by owning rental income; and how to make sure that buying real estate is not only profitable, but enjoyable as well. It is unlikely that you will find many investments that give you high returns, safety, tax benefits, and *cash flow* to match real estate. At the same time, you also need to be prepared for the interaction with tenants, complexities in recordkeeping and taxes, and the need to tie up capital for a longer period of time than with stock.

Studying the Rental Income Market

There is an old expression that "the market rewards patience." While this was aimed originally at stocks, it is equally true of real estate. In the Internet world, the stock market may punish patience and reward high-volume trades in some instances. But even with the Internet, real estate transactions usually still take a lot of time.

You may be able to narrow down your search using the Internet. Many sites offer not only references to local brokers and agents, but also current listings of property for sale. This means that you can study a range of potential properties without having to spend time with a real estate agent and be shown properties beyond your price range, out of your desired investment region, or otherwise inappropriate for your needs.

The method you employ at the very beginning of the process largely determines the quality of the properties you review. A common method for finding property, whether as a primary residence or for investment purposes, is to visit a local real estate office and speak to the agent on the floor. This is often done with no references, prequalification, or other tests. Even the process of looking at properties may be flawed. The agent is likely to show you only listings held by that brokerage firm, which can severely limit what you are shown, in terms of location, price, and features.

Valuable Resource

Online sites can link you to state-by-state professionals as well as actual current real estate listings. Check these sites as examples:

- http://www.imrmls.com:8080/servlet/IDisplayListings
- http://dmoz.org/Regional/North_America/United_States/
- http://www.realestateregional.com/

A wiser method (but one that requires more patience) is to begin by drawing up a list of features you need to know about before investing in property. These include:

1. *Price.* The first question on most people's minds is what properties cost. For some, this is limited to the question, How much do I need to make a down payment? It should extend far beyond this question, however. The evaluation of price should be made in context of typical prices in the area. Is this price a bargain? What are prices of similar homes in the same or nearby neighborhoods? Don't expect real estate agents to show you only the bargains; perform your own investigation.

2. *Location.* The location of the property is crucial to identifying properties that are likely to appreciate in value. Location extends not only to a specific neighborhood and its attributes, but also to the area of a town or city, economic status affecting real estate values, noise and other nuisances nearby, and availability of conveniences.

   neighborhood in transition
   an area in which the quality of housing, maintenance levels, appearance, and social trends such as crime levels are changing. In a positive transition, older homes are improved, renovated and updated in preparation for turnover to a new generation of owners. In a negative transition, lowered demand is characterized by empty and boarded-up homes, empty lots, and increased crime levels.

   A *neighborhood in transition* can be either a plus or a minus. If you observe areas over time, you notice that the makeup of a specific neighborhood changes. As a generation passes, properties are sold to new residents, older homes may be renovated, and new features added. This positive transition is a good sign that property values are going to rise as well. A negative transition occurs when residents stop maintaining properties, when low demand leads to empty or boarded-up houses, where empty lots are left for long periods because no one wants to build in that area, and where deleterious social trends like crime levels or gang activity are on the rise. In these areas, property values tend to decline, and while many bargains may be found, the long-term investment value is going to be questionable. Some investors specialize in buying and holding "distressed" properties; this is not a specialization most beginners will want to enter.

3. *Features.* The specific features you seek in a rental property should be defined by the demand for rentals itself. For example, the greatest

supply and demand

the driving forces of the real estate cycle, which includes three categories: financing, market, and rental. The supply of money determines interest rates, lender policies, and closing cost levels as well as the willingness of lenders to work with real estate investors. The supply of housing and demand for new housing determines pricing of residential property as well as how long it takes for properties to sell, whether they sell at full price or at a discount (or premium), and whether or not bargains can be found under present conditions. The level of supply and demand for rentals determines market rates as well as vacancy levels and trends.

return on investment may be found in one- and two-bedroom homes or duplex and triplex units; you may discover that four-bedroom homes do not yield adequate rents to cover your cash flow and expenses. This analysis is going to vary from one area to another; but it is important to analyze local features as a starting point. Compare market rates for rentals with different features to get an idea of how you can produce the best return on your investment.

4. *Age and condition.* What market are you interested in? Do you want a no-maintenance property that you can just rent out the day after the purchase is complete? Or do you seek a lower-priced bargain property that will require cosmetic improvements? The cost of properties will reflect the level of work you will need to do, so you should first define whether you are interested strictly in buying and holding rental property, or whether you want to buy, improve, and sell at a profit. There are many ways to approach the market, and defining your preferences is an important step to go through before you start putting offers on houses.

5. *Demand attributes.* One of the most overlooked steps in deciding whether to develop a rental income investment portfolio is a study of local *supply and demand* features. Demand comes in at least three forms: financing, market, and rental.

Financing demand refers to the availability of money to lend. When a lot of money is available, when rates are low, and when lenders want to find borrowers, they offer attractive closing cost terms, low rates, and fast review. When money is tight, borrowing will be more expensive. Interest rates will be higher, lenders will charge more *points*, and closing costs will have to be paid just to process the paperwork.

Market demand is reflected in the prices of real estate. The *real estate cycle* is similar to all cycles; it has up and down times. When demand is high—meaning there are more buyers than sellers—prices are driven up and builders cannot complete houses quickly enough. When demand is low—meaning there are more sellers than buyers—it takes longer for housing sales to be completed, sales take place at discount from the list price, and builders do not begin new projects. This cyclical tendency is illustrated in Figure 1.1.

The history of real estate prices reflects changes in demand over time. This is shown in the summary in Figure 1.2 However, demand itself is local. So the conditions reflected nationally will not necessarily apply to condition in your city or town.

This summary of housing prices demonstrates the strong and consistent nationwide market demand. Over many years, average sales price for residential property have climbing upward steadily, outpacing the rate of inflation during most years. The dollar values and percent of annual change are summarized in Table 1.1.

financing demand

the demand for money that can be used to lend in real estate transactions. As lenders' interest rates rise and fall, their policies and offers vary based on the money supply. When money is plentiful, rates are low and closing terms will be offered at attractive rates; when money is scarce, interest rates are higher and it will cost more to move through the borrowing process.

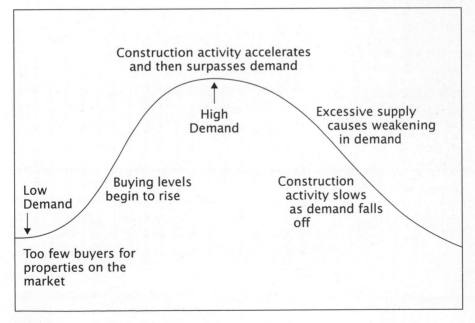

FIGURE 1.1　The real estate cycle.

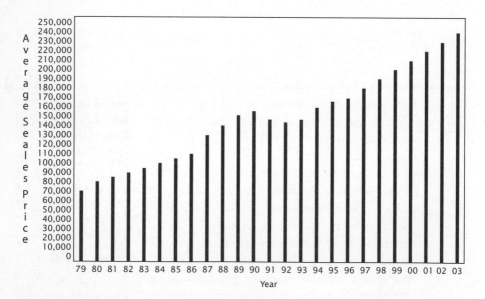

points

a cost of borrowing charged by lenders, equal to one percent of the amount to be borrowed. Also called "loan origination fees," points reflect the current availability of money to loan. When the money supply is plentiful, lenders tend to reduce fees, and when money is scarce, points and other fees tend to rise.

Note that average prices declined in only two out of the 25 years in the Table 1.1. This demonstrates the historical strength of real estate values.

Rental demand is the least understood of the three types. It is unrelated to the better-known market demand in an area. Because market demand is usually driven by purchasers who will live in the houses they buy, the trend in supply and demand is reflected by local employment statistics, lifestyle, and other social attributes. Rental demand is driven by the number of people who cannot afford to buy or—who do not want to buy—they want to rent. In some areas, market demand can be strong but rental demand weak. In other areas, the opposite is true. The important thing to remember is: Market and rental demand are driven by different forces. For example, in a city with a large college population, rental demand is likely to be high, at least while school terms are active. However, if the permanent population of the same area is primarily retired, market demand could be relatively low.

FIGURE 1.2 Average housing sales prices.

Source: U.S. Census Bureau

Table 1.1 Average Housing Sales Price

Year	Price	Change	Year	Price	Change
1979	$71,800	—	1992	$144,100	–2.1%
1980	76,400	6.4%	1993	147,000	2.5
1981	83,000	8.6	1994	154,500	4.6
1982	83,900	1.1	1995	158,700	2.7
1983	89,800	7.0	1996	166,400	4.9
1984	97,600	8.7	1997	176,200	5.9
1985	100,800	3.3	1998	181,900	3.2
1986	111,900	11.0	1999	195,600	7.5
1987	127,200	13.7	2000	207,000	5.8
1988	138,300	8.7	2001	213,200	3.0
1989	148,800	7.6	2002	228,700	7.3
1990	149,800	0.7	2003	244,800	7.0
1991	147,200	–1.7			

Source: U.S. Census Bureau

Valuable Resource

To check housing statistics and trends, check the U.S. Census Bureau Web site, at http://www.census.gov/.

6. *Financing.* In the stock market, it is relatively easy to get an investment program started. With a few thousand dollars, you can buy stocks directly—for as little as $100, you can open a mutual fund account. In real estate, cash investments are beyond most people's means, so the majority of equity value will be financed. This means that you have to address several questions in your initial analysis. Is your credit excellent? Good credit paves the way for more financing options, whereas a record of poor credit prevents many people from being able to get loans for a rental income program. Another question worth investigating is that of financing alternatives. Do local lenders offer a

market demand
the demand for property, reflected in price trends of housing; when demand rises, property prices rise as well, especially if housing is scarce. When an excess of housing is available, the demand levels off and prices flatten or decline.

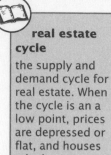

real estate cycle

the supply and demand cycle for real estate. When the cycle is an a low point, prices are depressed or flat, and houses take longer to sell; as the market demand begins to rise, more building activity occurs and prices rise.

rental demand

the current level of demand or the number of tenants seeking rentals versus the number of rental units available. Rental demand levels determine market rates as well as vacancy levels and duration.

variety of programs? Are rates attractive? (Rates for investment properties tend to be higher than for owner-occupied housing, and down payment requirements are likely to be higher as well.)

If commercial loans are not available, what other methods can you use? You could seek properties in which sellers will *carry* all or some of the debt. The problem here is that when sellers offer to finance a sale, it often means there is a serious problem with the structure. If the seller knows it is impossible to get conventional financing, that could be a troubling sign. You may be buying someone else's problems when you deal with seller-financed properties. At the very least, you would want to get an independent home inspection before agreeing to accept a seller's offer to carry a loan.

7. *Cash flow.* When you have analyzed all aspects of your local market, demand, financing, and other aspects, you end up with the most important question of all: Do the numbers work? In Chapter 2, we explore the importance of cash flow and show how to make these important calculations. It is essential for you to determine whether cash flow is practical in your situation. For example, if you expect to make monthly mortgage payments of $1,100 per month but market rates for rents are only $500, it is obvious that cash flow doesn't work out. And it is not as simple as comparing rents to mortgage payments.

Valuable Resource

To whom do you go to find an independent home inspector? Stay away from contractors who will also offer to perform work or refer work to someone they know. Ethical home inspectors refuse to perform repair work or offer referrals. Use an inspector who is a member of the American Society of Home Inspectors (ASHI). To review performance standards and to find a qualified inspector in your area, check the ASHI home page at http://www.ashi.org/.

You also need to consider nonmortgage expenses and payments; tax benefits; and the possibility of vacancies. How much cushion do you have between your monthly family income and expenses? If unexpected expenses or a period of vacancies would cause a disaster in your finances, you need to evaluate that realistically, and consider whether it makes sense to invest in rental income. Some alternatives include higher down payments (translating to lower monthly mortgage levels), seeking less expensive properties or multiunit properties, where

carry
taking a loan on property; when a seller agrees to carry the loan, it means the seller transfers title to the buyer and then takes on the role of lender.

the ratio between income and mortgage expense may be more favorable, or simply waiting until your financial picture is stronger. It makes sense to identify risks now, before you invest money, so that you know what risks you may face after you have closed on a rental property.

Advantages to Long-Term Investing

You may divide your investment into classification on several criteria: risk level, dollar amount allocation, or type of investment, are examples. You can also distinguish between investments by how long you plan to hold them. Traditionally, real estate has been thought of as a long-term investment, whereas stocks can be either short term or long term. This distinction has much to do with the *liquidity* levels of each market. You can buy and sell stocks or mutual fund shares with a telephone call and the transaction can be completed in seconds. Real estate purchases, in comparison, are expensive, complex, and take time. By this distinction alone, the cost of completing a real estate transaction makes the entire market far different than stocks. One advantage to real estate investing is that its long-term characteristics provide stability and safety, attributes that appeal to most investors. In spite of the illiquidity of the market, your inability to buy and sell real estate quickly or easily provides discipline to your long-term investment program and may be well suited to your personal financial goals.

Price appreciation is a second way to distinguish between investments, and also a second form of advantage to real estate investing. Both the stock market and real estate have performed well over the long term. However, stocks tend to go through highly volatile price cycles. Investors have often experienced months and, in some instances, several years in which prices were depressed or

liquidity

a market condition referring to the ease of buying and selling, or the availability of cash. A highly liquid market (like the stock market) allows investors to move cash in and out of positions cheaply and quickly. Illiquid markets (like directly owned real estate) require complex and expensive closings to buy and sell investments; or refinancing or additional mortgages to remove cash.

volatility

a measurement of market risk; the tendency for market value to changes gradually over time (low volatility) or to change erratically and unpredictably (high volatility).

erratic. The same economic forces leading to stock market instability have also affected real estate values, but by no means as drastically. Figure 1.2 made this point; Census Bureau statistics make the case that on average, residential property values move upward with reassuring consistency. So while both stocks and real estate offer long-term price appreciation to investors, *volatility*—the tendency for market values to remain consistent over time (low volatility) or to change unexpectedly in either direction (high volatility)—can be viewed as one way to measure *market risk*. The low volatility of real estate, in comparison to stocks, makes it a safer long-term investment.

Another advantage to generating rental income is that, over a long period of time, rent-paying tenants provide funds to pay down your mortgage. The often-observed point that "your tenant pays your mortgage" is simplistic because, in fact, you also take on many risks when you create a large debt and come to depend on tenants to provide the cash flow you need. There is much more to it. However, assuming that you are aware of those risks and that you pick tenants and screen them diligently, the regular cash flow produced by tenants makes financed real estate viable.

Financing real estate is seen by many as a large risk. You may carry debt as high as 70 or 80 percent of property value in the form of a mortgage, and you require rental income to keep up with those payments. As with all forms of risk, there is an associated advantage. Using a relatively small down payment and financing the majority of your investment basis is a popular form of *leverage*, which is the use of a small amount of money to control a much more valuable asset. Just as some stock market investors use margin accounts to increase their stock positions, real estate investors borrow money to leverage and, thus, to afford to purchase property to produce rental income. The concept of leverage depends on building equity value over the long term to build wealth. Rental income generated by tenants is applied to *debt service*, the monthly payments you are required to make to the lender, including principal and interest and, when applicable, *impounds* as well. When impounds are included, the total of monthly payments is referred to as *PITI* (principal, interest, taxes, insurance).

Among the advantage to investing in rental income property, one of the most significant is the income tax benefit it provides. Most investors are not allowed to deduct losses in many forms of investments, except to offset them against gains in other investments (see Chapter 7 for the details). Real estate investors are given a special provision in federal tax law allowing them to deduct up to $25,000 of losses each year, subject to some limitations. They can depreciate the buildings they purchase and also deduct mortgage interest, property taxes, utilities, insurance, and other expenses necessary for operating a rental income program. The tax benefits are significant; it is often possible to report a yearly loss for tax purposes while also generating more cash coming in than you are paying out. So the tax benefits also affect after-tax cash flow, often making the difference between practical and impractical in your investment program.

Yet another benefit in buying real estate is the fact that its value can be insured. In fact, your lender is going to require that you carry insurance to protect against fire and other possible damages to your rental income property. You cannot insure stock market investments in the same way. Stock market investors face the possibility of sudden and unexpected loss on a daily basis; real estate investors face the remote possibility of loss but their equity is protected through insurance coverage.

When you own rental income property, you also achieve an important form of *diversification* in your portfolio. The basic idea of diversifying is to spread capital among several dissimilar investments so that, in the event you lose in one, you will not lose in all. Stocks and real estate are perfect examples. There is a tendency for investment capital to move back and forth between stocks and real estate depending on a number of economic conditions and trends, most notably prevailing interest rates. Diversification itself can be achieved within one market by placing money in many different

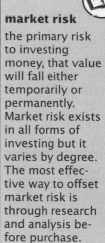

market risk
the primary risk to investing money, that value will fall either temporarily or permanently. Market risk exists in all forms of investing but it varies by degree. The most effective way to offset market risk is through research and analysis before purchase.

leverage
the use of capital to control or to purchase assets worth far more; rental income is applied to paying the cost of leveraged capital, specifically its debt service.

debt service
payments to a lender required each month, consisting of principal and interest and, if applicable, impounds for property taxes and insurance.

impounds

amounts included in a monthly mortgage payment beyond principal and interest, required under the terms of some mortgage contracts. Typical impounds are collected monthly for property taxes and insurance. The lender then makes periodic payments for those obligations.

PITI

a term describing a monthly mortgage payment that includes all four elements: principal, interest, taxes, and insurance.

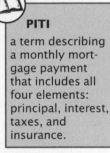

diversification

a method for reducing risk by placing capital in several different products; the purpose is to avoid a large loss if and when economic conditions cause price declines in a particular market sector.

areas. For example, a stock market investor is advised to own shares of many different types of stocks that operate in dissimilar economic cycles, to avoid a portfolio-wide threat of loss. A more advanced form of diversification is *asset allocation*, a method of selecting investments in several different areas to reduce the economic risks even further. Asset allocation is really a broader form of diversification. The distinction is that a diversified portfolio may exist solely in the stock market or in real estate; asset allocation, on the other hand, usually involves placing percentages of investment capital in several different areas: stocks, real estate, cash reserves, personal retirement funds, insurance with cash value or annuities, or precious metals, for example.

In a diversified investment portfolio, you not only spread risks; you also create dissimilar investment features. In stocks, relatively small dividend payments do not usually represent a lot of current income unless you own a large portfolio of stocks. In comparison, rental income generates substantial monthly cash flow, and this is both necessary and an important advantage. You need the cash flow to cover your mortgage obligation (debt service) and also to maintain the property. So cash flow is actually more critical than net income or loss for tax purposes, because it determines whether or not you can afford to buy and hold real estate. Chapter 2 examines the whole issue of cash flow in detail.

A final point worth mentioning in the list of advantages is that of personal control. To many real estate investors, this is the most attractive feature of all. When you buy shares of stock, you own a small piece of a larger equity in a corporation; but you have no voice in the day-to-day management decisions. The executives and board of directors decide whether to acquire or merge with other companies, which products or services to promote or to abandon, and when to buy or sell capital assets. These are important decisions that define profit and loss; but the individual stockholder is only going along for the ride, hoping that those shares of stock grow in value. Whether or not that happens depends on how well management makes those important decisions. In comparison, when you buy a rental income property, *you* are your own management and board of directors. You decide when to buy or sell properties, how much rent to charge, and who you will accept as tenants. You set policies regarding maintenance; if you do the minimum, property will deteriorate and value will follow, and if you keep property in excellent shape you will experience increased value and more responsible tenants. This personal control is the single feature that will determine, more than anything else, how well your investment appreciates in comparison to other property in the same neighborhood.

> **asset allocation**
> an expansion of investment diversification, in which percentages of total capital are invested in dissimilar types of investments, such as stocks, real estate, or cash deposits.

Disadvantages to Long-Term Investing

Just as every form of investment has advantages, it also has disadvantages. This is as true of real estate as of any other choice. In fact, some of the advantages listed in the preceding section have a corresponding disadvantage. You should be aware of these features of a particular investment before deciding to proceed with an investment program, whether you are considering stocks, real estate, a combination, or some other product.

In real estate, one of the most significant disadvantages is the long-term cost of buying property. Mortgage payments have to be made every month, even when property is vacant or when tenants are late with the rent. In the earlier years of a long-term mortgage, the majority of the monthly payment goes to interest. This cost is far higher than most people realize. For example, if you borrow $100,000 and finance your investment with a 30-year loan at 6.25 percent, your monthly payment will be $615.72. Over the full term of the loan, your payments will add up to $221,659.20, more than twice the amount you borrowed. So the "real cost" of buying that property has to take interest into account.

The true cost of your home comes into focus when you also consider how long it takes to pay down the principal balance of the mortgage. The 6.25 percent loan will be less than 7 percent paid off at the end of the fifth year; the rest of the payments are all interest. In fact, it takes 21 years to pay off one-half of the entire mortgage. Because of the way that interest is calculated each month (based on the outstanding loan balance) the amount you owe declines very slowly at first, and only gradually accelerates in the last 10 years of the 30-year period.

Even when tenants cover the cost of financing rental income property, the true cost is significant. It is quite possible and even likely that the impressive gains in market value over many years will go primarily to interest payments. This means the lender really makes money on real estate, and the investor does not. Look at some numbers. If you had purchased a home in 1979, the average price nationally would have been $71,800 (see Table 1.1, Census Bureau information). If you put down $11,800 and financed $60,000 at the typical 1979 market rate for investment property of 12 percent, your monthly payment on a 30-year loan would have been $617.17. Assuming you did not refinance that debt, by the end of 2004, 25 years later, you would have paid a total of $185,151 and your remaining balance on your loan would be $13,872. So the total of payments consists of $139,023 in interest and $46,128 in principal. At that point, you would have paid the original purchase price of the property 2.5 times over. Of course, the transaction would involve tax benefits as well as tenant payments of rent, so is this a fair analysis? Yes. It is not the complete analysis, but it makes the point that rental income property is more expensive than the simple purchase price. In fact, the *real* cost of the property has to involve a calculation of purchase price, plus interest, minus net rental income, minus tax benefits. And then you would have to calculate the annual average return. The point to be made is that financing the majority of your investment does not produce profits that can be judged easily. Returning to the example of a property purchased in 1979 for $71,800, based on national averages, what would that property be worth 25 years later? According to the Census Bureau, the average value at the end of 2003 was $244,800. If we perform a simple calculation comparing market appreciation to the cost of borrowing, we discover:

Current market value	$244,800
Minus: original purchase price	−71,800
Minus: Interest, 25 years	−139,023
Profit	$ 33,977

To take this calculation a step farther, examine the rate of return. You originally made a down payment of $11,800, which was the amount of capital you had to put into the investment. Your overall profit over 25 years was $22,177, or an average of $887 per year. That works out to approximately 4.3 percent compounded over those years:

$$[1.043\% \times \$11,800]^{25} = \$33,806$$

$$\$33,806 - \$11,800 = \$22,006$$

The stock market averages about 7 percent per year in comparison. So a stock market investment in 1979 would have produced *average* returns adding up to $64,044, or a profit of $52,244. The comparison between return on a real estate investment and the stock market is shown in Figure 1.3.

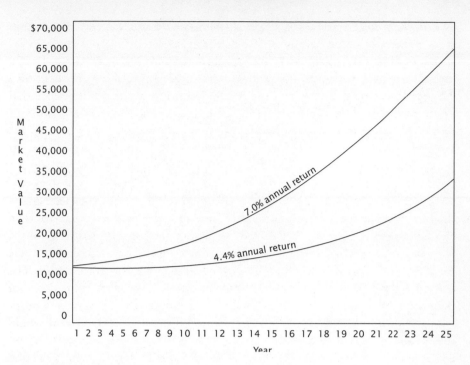

FIGURE 1.3 Comparison of a 25-year compound return.

This analysis is incomplete; it only shows the different values between the two markets. It does not consider the importance of cash flow (tenants paying rents to cover mortgages) or tax benefits, which can be significant in real estate. Even so, the point is worth making: Investments in real estate cannot be judged by comparing purchase price to sales price; there is much more involved in that calculation.

A valid comparison of the true rate of return in rental income property, versus the stock market, does not take all the variables into consideration. The purpose to this comparative exercise is to demonstrate that in fact, you cannot simply compare market rate increases without also keeping the *cost* of ownership in mind. The varying costs and benefits change the equation. As long as rental income is adequate to cover all of the costs, the real final outcome over many years is going to be based on how successfully the investment builds wealth. The value to having rents is that they offset interest costs, so that the effect is as close as possible to zero. This means that for no year-to-year growth in your tax liabilities (and often, a decline in liability) you gradually build equity from market appreciation as well as from slowly reducing your mortgage debt level. The overall real cost of purchase can be reduced in several ways, including:

- Replacing original mortgages with lower-rate mortgages as market rates fall
- Using high down payments to reduce long-term interest costs
- Contracting for faster pay-off terms of the mortgage
- Accelerating mortgage payments

These ideas are explained and examined in greater detail in Chapter 8. Looking beyond the long-term cost of real estate, it is equally important to compare markets in terms of liquidity. Real estate is an illiquid market, especially compared to the stock market. To get money out of your real estate investment, you have only three alternatives. These are:

1. Sell the property.
2. Refinance and take out cash.
3. Find a source for a second mortgage or equity line of credit.

The illiquidity of the real estate market is more severe for rental property than for your own home. Interest rates are usually higher for investment property, and most lenders also require a higher down payment. You may be able to finance your home for 10 percent down, sometimes even less. But for investment property, you could be required to put as much as 30 percent down. It may also be difficult if not impossible to take cash out upon refinancing investment property, if only because the lender's risks are much greater for investment property than for your primary residence. Finally, while people with good credit can easily find an equity line of credit, the majority of lenders will not grant these lines to anyone except owner-occupied housing. All of these rules add to the illiquidity of real estate, so realistically, you need to appreciate the long-term nature of real estate as well as the restrictions on accessing equity.

In the preceding section, we discussed cash flow as an advantage. The tenant-generated rents should be adequate to make mortgage payments and cover maintenance. However, the question of cash flow can also work as a disadvantage. Vacancies, nonpayment of rent, and unexpected maintenance expenses all add to the burden of owning real estate and you need to be able to afford a period of unexpected demands on your cash. If your family income is barely adequate to cover your expenses, an unexpected loss of rental income, even if only for a month or two, could be financially catastrophic to your personal budget. If that margin is too close, rental income property may be too high-risk right now. You might need to wait until you have more flexibility in your budget, or until you can create a savings cushion in the event the cash flow stops or maintenance expenses come up.

Every landlord knows that among the *potential* risks of owning rental income property, tenants can turn a positive one into a negative, and very suddenly. For many people, this factor alone has prevented them from embarking on an otherwise profitable real estate investment venture. There are ways to minimize risks, however. It is not necessary to avoid rental income altogether.

Stock investors know that the more advance research they perform, the less chance they will make a mistake in picking stocks. So they study financial statements, watch earnings trends, and even chart stock price movements. In real estate, you need to do the same advance analysis, not only to pick the right properties and to identify the strongest possible markets, but also to find the very best tenants. This means that you need to go through several steps when tenants apply for consideration. These include:

1. *Use a detailed rental application form.* Use a detailed rental application including bank account numbers, current tenant address, current and past landlord contact information, and permission to check credit (and collect a fee to cover the cost of the credit check). If the tenant does not complete and sign the form or cannot provide you with *all* of the required information, reject the application. There are good reasons why applicants will not give you landlord's phone numbers, for example.

2. *Check* all *references thoroughly.* Once you have the completed form in hand, get in touch with both current and previous landlord and ask them for details about their experiences with the applicant. The past landlord contact is important; current landlords might leave out important information because they want the tenant out. An ex-landlord will be more candid about what kind of tenant the person was.

   If the tenant lives locally, drive by the current address and see how the property looks. Has the tenant taken good care of the property? Or is landscaping in disarray and junk thrown out on the lawn? If you accept a tenant, the appearance of their current house or apartment is what your place will look like in a few months.

   Also call current employers and verify that the person is employed there. If a tenant does not have a job, why would you rent your property to them? How will they pay rent? If the tenant does not put down accurate information concerning employer, monthly income, or other details on the rental application, that is a red flag. Also verify the existence of a current bank account. When applicants are unable to provide you with a bank reference, it could mean they are avoiding liens or judgments or have other money problems.

3. *Also check credit history and local criminal history.* Get a current credit report using the tenant's payment, and read it carefully. Such reports may list judgments, evictions, bankruptcies and other problems you should know about, and the credit report is the place to start. You can also check with your county's Superior Court for any criminal convictions. This is public information. In most counties, all you need to do is go to the court clerk's office and ask whether any convictions have been recorded, and provide the applicant's name. For example, if an applicant has been convicted for operating a "meth lab," you would not want to rent out your house to that person.

4. *Use a printed rental contract form for complies with your state's laws.* Always use a printed rental contract that spells out all of the terms and conditions of the rental agreement. You are usually better off renting *month-to-month* rather than entering into a lease. The one-year lease usually protects tenants more than landlords and may bring up many problems if the tenant turns out to be less than perfect.

5. *Require a security deposit as well as first and last months' rent.* Protect yourself by collecting enough cash up front so that, in the event of damages to your property, or nonpayment of rent, you have some flexibility in dealing with the tenant. Some landlords are sympathetic to those who cannot afford first and last plus a security deposit; but when tenants are not asked to pay up front, problems can arise. For example, if tenants decide to give notice, they may simply fail to pay the next month's rent, reasoning that the security deposit can be converted to a rent payment. However, if they damage property or do not clean the place, then you are going to end up losing money as a consequence.

6. *Complete a statement of condition with the tenant present.* As part of the process of moving a tenant into your property, walk through with the tenant and complete a very detailed statement of condition, noting any and all defects, condition of walls, carpets, any furniture, appliances, and fixtures. Both you and the tenant should sign the form and each gets a copy. This solves problems that may arise when the tenancy ends. You may claim the tenant depreciated the place, and the tenant may argue that the damage existed when he or she moved in. The statement of condition, signed by landlord and tenant, resolves the disagreement.

7. *Enforce all of your rules regarding rent payments and more.* Having a written contract protects you; however, the conditions have to be enforced. So you need to make sure the tenant does not move extra people into the property beyond those names listed on the application. If you have a no-pets policy, don't allow the tenant to get a puppy or a cat later on. If the tenant is supposed to keep the lawn mowed and does not, give

the tenant a choice: Either do the work or you will raise their rent to cover the cost of hiring someone else to do it. In other words, you have a contract that both sides signed; make sure the tenant follows the rules.

8. *Check the property frequently.* One step a lot of rental income property investors overlook is the importance of monitoring tenants. This does not mean you have the right to enter the property without good reason or without notice; you do not. But you should drive by the property frequently. Danger signs include many cars parked at the house, high levels of traffic, garbage, or appliances in the yard, and other signs of the property being poorly maintained.

> **month-to-month**
> a type of rental agreement in which landlord and tenant continue the rental from one month to the next. In comparison, a lease binds both sides for the entire lease period.

Also give neighbors your name and address and tell them you are renting out the property. Invite them to contact you if they have any complaints concerning noise levels or unusual activity. Check out any complaints promptly. If you find that the tenants are disturbing their neighbors, tell them the problem has to stop immediately. If it does not stop, give them notice. If you have good reason to believe tenants are breaking the law (i.e., manufacturing or selling drugs from your property) contact the police and tell them your concerns.

There is a tendency for first-time investors to assume that tenants and houses cannot be distinguished by type. But in fact, a particular type of house is going to attract a particular type of tenant. For example, a very modern house located in a suburban neighborhood is likely to attract families, whereas smaller, more remote units are more likely to attract single people or young married couples. The rent level, condition and age of the property, and proximity to services and conveniences, will all determine the mix of tenants who are likely to be interested in renting the property. This is an important point in how well you are going to interact with your tenants. As a general rule, the better the condition of the property, the better the mix of tenants will be; this does not ensure that a well-maintained home will always attract responsible, fair-minded tenants. It just improves the odds.

A final point about tenants: You have to determine whether you are suited to dealing with other people. Investing in rental income properties requires that you be willing to deal with occasional problems and perhaps even confrontations. You have to expect telephone calls for petty complaints on evenings and weekends, and the unexpected catastrophe. For example, your water heater may burst on Sunday evening, so you will need to know where the shut-off valve is located. And the top priority the next morning will be to find a plumber who can install a new water heater that day. Tenants may call you late at night because the sliding door is stuck or because they think they hear a noise outside. You may need to place an answering machine on your telephone. In fact, many landlords pay for a second line specifically so that they can screen calls and have control over when they respond to tenants.

To some people, these minor annoyances go with the territory and they take it in stride. For others, the never-ending intrusion makes the entire venture a big hassle, and they conclude that they are not cut out for landlording. One solution is to sell and get out; another would be to place properties under professional management. Local companies provide services including fielding tenant complaints, filling vacancies and checking applicant references, and even paying bills and keeping books, usually for about 10 percent of monthly rents collected. For some people, the ability to not deal with tenants directly is well worth the management expense.

Deciding When to Sell

Every investor, whether holding real estate or other investments, constantly faces the problem of knowing how to time a sale correctly. The question depends on your personal investing goals as well as market price trends. For example, if you intend to hold onto property to build equity for your retirement, it would make sense to keep that property (or exchange it for another) until retirement age. If you want to dispose of property more quickly, when is the best time? When the price of your rental income property has risen, it is likely that the entire market has risen as well. If you intend to transfer investment capital from one property to another, you face three problems in this situation: properties are generally going to be high, you will be taxed on your gain when you sell, and there are costs involved in selling one property and buying another.

With these problems in mind, you need to know before you buy property how long you intend to keep it. That goal will be affected by several unknown elements, including:

- Your discovery that you do not enjoy working with tenants
- The realization that in a particular case, cash flow is not strong enough
- Changes in the market leading to weak demand for rentals
- Your decision to move capital from real estate into other investments
- The realization that the level of work required is too high

Market timing is only one aspect of when you will want to sell. For most people who go into rental income investments, the hands-on aspects of the venture are appealing and highly satisfying; but some people simply do not realize how much work is involved or what it is like to have to manage cash flow, until they actually buy and operate property. In situations where your dissatisfaction or risk level is simply too great, selling makes sense—even if that means cutting losses instead of making profits.

In timing a sale, you face the same problems you face in the stock market. In a market where prices have risen dramatically, you hesitate, thinking prices might continue to rise. No one wants to miss out on more profits. In fact, the temptation at those times is to put *more* capital into real estate so that your future profits will be even higher. When markets are moving up, there is a tendency to believe the trend is permanent. This belief is wrong, but it is widely believed.

In a market where prices have flattened out or fallen, investors also tend to believe that the profitability of real estate is over, and permanently; that profitable growth will never return; and that the decision to invest in real estate was ill-advised. Many people sell at such times, to later realize that the timing of their decision was a mistake. At the height of despair among investors, it is likely that the next run-up in values is about to begin. This has happened over and over and will happen again in the future.

To overcome these normal investor attitudes and take control of your investment policies, set specific goals. Your goals may be structured in one of several statements, such as:

1. I will sell this property when it has doubled in market value.
2. I will sell in 10 years, no matter what price changes have occurred.
3. I will hold onto this property as long as it is paying for itself (meaning that rents are adequate to cover all expenses and debt service).
4. I will continue investing in rental income property as long as rental demand remains at or above current levels (expressed as a percentage, for example).

One problem in selling a specific property and replacing it with another is the tendency for real estate trends to occur locally. In other words, the trends you experience in one property are likely to be typical of the entire market in your city or town. You probably want to restrict your activity to rentals within your immediate area, because absentee landlording raises many more problems. So property values tend to be universal within a specific region.

If you want to dispose of one property and invest capital elsewhere, a sensible approach is to change the type of property. For example, single-family housing tends to increase in value better than most other residential properties; but multiunit rentals usually produce far better cash flow. So you might sell a single-family house and replace it with a duplex or triplex, to improve cash flow. A more ambitious idea would be to buy an apartment building.

These alternatives to outright sale can make sense when you are discouraged about cash flow or attributes of a particular property. When you are thinking of selling ask yourself: Do I want to sell because selling suits my long-term goals? Or is it because I am having problems with this property, a particular tenant, or the area where the property is located? The answer should determine whether or need to replace the property, or just move capital into other investments.

The Positive Long-Term Experience: A Matter of Management

Multiple Listing Service (MLS)

a subscription service available to real estate agents reporting all homes currently on the market. The MLS also includes valuable statistics about the current state of supply and demand in the market.

spread

the difference between asked and sales price of homes, expressed as a percentage. Example: Average homes were priced at $107,500 in the past year, and average sales prices were $102,300, a difference of $5,200. The spread is 4.8% ($5,200 ÷ $107,500).

With some sound preliminary research, you can create a positive long-term experience in managing your own rental income property. Invariably, people run into problems because they skipped one of the important steps to good management. There are five of these key steps:

1. *Investigate markets and market values in advance of buying.* Never trust a real estate agent to tell you how strong the market is today. Agents are always going to claim that the market is good; that is their job. Agents want to encourage you to buy, and they will invariably believe that today is a "good time" to pick up a property. You need to investigate on your own. Gather *MLS* data from a real estate agent or local banker and study it yourself. Look for the key indicators. These include the *spread*, the difference between asked and sales price; how long a property was on the market before it sold; and the current *inventory* of residential property for sale. The lower the spread, the shorter the time on the market, and the smaller the current inventory, the better the indicators are. All of this information should be available from real estate and banking institutions in your area, and MLS data usually include these statistics.

2. *Look for good bargains in market value and potential rental value.* When you buy stocks, you are wise to check the fundamentals: revenue and earnings, capital strength, and more. The same is true for real estate. Before deciding to buy, you need to check the

real estate fundamental indicators in your area. These include market price trends, the demand for rental units (often expressed in *occupancy rate*), and a comparison between market rent levels and the mortgage payment you will have to pay.

3. *Screen tenants thoroughly and check all reference.* Never accept a tenant who cannot provide references or whose references are poor. The importance of carefully screening tenants cannot be emphasized too much. Use a form requiring current address, bank, employer, and current and past landlords. Check all of these references. If an applicant is not willing or is unable to provide the information, that should end the process. If any references are negative, reject the applicant.

4. *Enter month-to-month rental agreements rather than leases.* In typical situations where you, as an individual, are going to rent a single-family house or multifamily units (duplex or triplex, for example), you have an advantage in using a month-to-month agreement. This allows you to give notice without going through the complex steps of breaking a lease. While leases can be broken for good cause, it is complicated. Some people argue that a lease is preferable because to commits a tenant to a full year. But in a case of nonpayment of rent, you probably will not be able to get full restitution, whether using a lease or month-to-month agreement.

5. *Calculate cash flow including tax benefits.* Never purchase real estate without first going through a complete calculation of cash flow. This has to be done on a realistic basis, including tax benefits and all forms of payment you will have to make. The calculation involves several steps, but it is not as complicated as some people believe. (See Chapter 2 for a detailed step-by-step explanation of how to calculate cash flow.)

inventory
the homes currently on the market, expressed both in number of properties and months' of availability. For example, today there are 206 properties for sale. Typically, 38 homes are sold per month. There is a 5.4 month inventory available (206 ÷ 38).

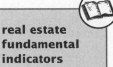

real estate fundamental indicators
the market facts that define whether it is prudent to invest in real estate. These indicators include supply and demand and its effect on current prices; levels of demand for rental real estate units; the cost of borrowing money to finance a purchase; and a comparison between market rates you expect to receive and debt service and other payments you will be required to make.

occupancy rate
the level of occupancy, expressed as a percentage. For example, a rental property was occupied 10.5 months last year. Occupancy rate was 87.5% (10.5 ÷ 12). On a statistical level, all rentals indicate the local trend. For example, in your area, a total of 1,462 units exist and currently, 1,391 are occupied. The occupancy rate is 95.1% (1,391 ÷ 1,462). This statistic is often expressed as "vacancy rate," which is the opposite, or the percentage of available rental space not occupied.

The whole point of going through the preliminary steps is to avoid mistakes. Discovering an error after you have purchased real estate is the expensive way to go, but spending time and effort on the fundamental preliminary steps will save you thousands of dollars in the long run.

The next chapter provides a detailed explanation of how to calculate and control rental income property cash flow.

2

Financial Aspects
Keeping the Cash Flowing

For many investors, the financial questions are the most troubling. The complexities of figuring out mortgage payments, taxes, and accounting require knowledge and skill; so there is a tendency to skip over these areas and to depend on experts to take care of the details.

This is a mistake. To make the basic decision about purchasing rental income property, you must assess the financial side of things and be able to decide—ahead of time—whether the idea even works out in terms of cash flow.

The good news: These calculations are not as difficult as you think. It is really just a matter of deciding if the overall equation works out. Ideally, you want more cash coming in than going out. It would be even better if, in that *positive cash flow* situation, you could also claim a loss on your income tax return, reducing overall taxes as well. And this is not only possible; it is also *likely*. That is the powerful aspect of real estate: The creation of positive cash flow *and* tax benefits at the same time.

This chapter explores the various financial aspects of the decision to invest in rental income property: the concept of leverage, the relationship between rental income and mortgage payments, a detailed example of computing cash flow, computing mortgage breakdowns, and the various alternatives to financing your rental income property purchase.

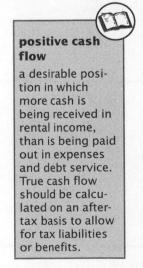

positive cash flow

a desirable position in which more cash is being received in rental income, than is being paid out in expenses and debt service. True cash flow should be calculated on an after-tax basis to allow for tax liabilities or benefits.

Leverage and Real Estate

The use of leverage in rental income property is unavoidable for most people. Investors cannot generally afford to pay cash for the entire value, so they have to finance their purchase. In the ideal situation, the amount of rental income generated through ownership of the property, will be adequate to pay for (1) debt service of the mortgage loan; (2) nondeductible costs such as *capital improvements*; (3) utilities, taxes, insurance, and other recurring expenses; and (4) unexpected expenses such as periodic maintenance and repairs.

capital improvements

all changes made to land including the building itself and, following purchase, costs such as additions, a new roof, and other costs that are above and beyond the normal expenses of the property, such as repairs and maintenance.

investment risk

any form of risk you accept as part of how your investments are structured. In the case of rental income investments, the need for leverage adds risk, because you depend on rental income to be able to afford monthly mortgage payments.

When you borrow money to buy property, you leverage part of your purchase. In most cases, you will finance more than half of the total value. Typically, investment property requires 30 percent down payment; but some lenders will allow you to make smaller down payments. As an important point to remember, the more money you put down, the better your cash flow. This is true because the smaller your mortgage loan, the smaller your monthly payment. When the rental income is close to the same amount as the mortgage payment, it leaves little room for payment of other expenses. Cash flow, therefore, is directly related to the cost of property and the rental income that you derive from it as well as to the down payment you make when you buy the property.

The use of leverage in your investment portfolio also increases your *investment risk*. Whenever you borrow money to buy an investment property, you depend on rental income to make your monthly payments. So events like unexpected repairs, long periods of vacancy, or nonpayment of rent by tenants, add to that risk. If it were possible to own rental income property free and clear, most of the rental income would be clear profit, and the risk would be greatly reduced. For most investors, however, this desirable situation is seldom if ever achieved. The fact is most rental income property investments are based on leverage, often permanently.

Any time investment risk increases you have to contend with a number of other risks as well. In the case of rental income property, you hope that market values will grow fast enough so that you can earn a profit within the timeframe you pick. For example, if you believe it will take five years for your property value to increase enough to justify a sale, you are assuming certain facts about supply and demand. During that five-year period, you require adequate flow to continue to be able to afford mortgage payments and other expenses. If the market value does not increase adequately within the five-year period, you have to decide what to do. What if mortgage payments are falling short? That means you have to make up the difference out of your personal household budget. Do you continue in this way hoping for growth in the future? Or do you cut your losses now and get out? In assessing a negative cash flow situation in deciding whether or not to sell your rental income property, you need to compare potential income from other investments, to what you are earning or losing today. For example, if you believe that your rental property is growing in value by an average of 5 percent per year, are you making a net profit or losing money? If you have other investment capital in the stock market and mutual funds, where they are earning an average of 11 percent per year, what does this mean? To the extent that you have to put cash into your rental income property each month, you are losing the difference. If you have to invest an additional $5,000 per year just to cover your rental income property expenses, you need to go through a calculation to judge the lost value of that money. If your rental property originally cost you $90,000, this calculation would be:

Original cost of property	$90,000
5% average return	$4,500
Negative cash flow paid per year	$5,000
Lost stock market income, 11%	−550
Net return, real estate	$3,950
True net return ($3,950 ÷ $90,000)	4.4%

In this calculation, we consider the lost income you could be earning in the stock market, if the $5,000 negative cash flow was available to invest; and then reduce the average real estate yield by the lost income. This makes the comparison valid. You are making a net of 4.4 percent per year in real estate, compared to 11 percent average return in stocks. Diversification aside, in this situation you would be better off to cut your losses. In fact, your negative cash flow of $5,000 per year exceeds the average annual growth in value in real estate; so the investment is not only underperforming, it is also keeping capital tied up with no immediate prospects to outperform your other investment choices.

This dismal outcome is not typical. Real estate often performs far better than the return in the example. A $5,000 annual negative cash flow is very poor. And the 11 percent return in the stock market is not a reliable or a typical return, either. The example makes the point that a reliable comparison has to consider all elements: cash invested, market value, annual growth, and cash flow.

Mortgage Payments and Rental Income

The relationship between the level of rent you receive and the amount you pay for your mortgage is the key to cash flow or, at the very least, the starting point. You need to ensure that your rental income is adequate to pay your mortgage. So an initial test at the time you are thinking of buying a property is to quickly compare these two.

For example, if you are looking at a single-family house that costs $150,000 and you are going to put $45,000 down, your mortgage payment over 30 years, at 6.25 percent, will be $646.50. If market rents for such properties are only $600 per month, this investment does not make sense. Your initial negative cash flow is going to be $46.50 per month, before even calculating what you will have to pay for property taxes, insurance, utilities, and recurring maintenance—not to mention unexpected expenses. This comparison also leaves no room for the occasional vacancy. This example shows that on the basis of cash flow, that particular property is not a viable investment. You have to either look for less expensive properties or come up with a way to increase your down payment. If you were able to reduce your mortgage balance from $105,000 down to $90,000, your monthly payment would fall to $554.15. This is a much more likely mortgage obligation level given the market rents. You still need to figure out what other obligations come with the property to decide whether you can afford it.

Even knowing your monthly mortgage level, it is necessary to be able to break down the payment between interest and principal. You need this to complete

---

Valuable Resource

You can figure out the required monthly mortgage payment using one of numerous online calculators. Simply enter the amount to be borrowed, the interest rate and the number of years, and the monthly payment is automatically calculated. Search the Web on the words "mortgage" and "calculator" or use one of these Web sites:

- http://www.mortgage-calc.com/mortgage/simple.php
- http://mortgages.interest.com/content/calculators/monthly-payment.asp
- http://www.bankrate.com/brm/mortgage-calculator.asp

your calculations of cash flow, because the interest portion of your payment is deductible on your tax return. So to figure out tax benefits, you need to be able to estimate the total interest per year; this changes as your outstanding balance declines. The steps for calculating the breakdown from one month to another are shown in the following list, accompanied by the preceding example, a $105,000 loan for 30 years and a monthly payment of $646.50 with a 6.25 percent interest rate, as illustrated in the equations:

1. Revise the stated percentage rate to decimal form; divide the stated annual percentage by 100:

$$6.25\% \div 100 = 0.0625$$

2. Multiply the decimal equivalent in step 1 by the outstanding loan balance to arrive at the annual interest.

$$0.0625 \times \$105,000 = \$6,562.50$$

3. Divide the annual interest by 12 (months) to find this month's interest expense:

$$\$6,562.50 \div 12 = \$546.88$$

4. Subtract this month's interest from the total monthly payment to find this month's principal payment.

$$\$646.50 - \$546.88 = \$99.62$$

5. Subtract this month's principal payment from the outstanding loan balance to find the new outstanding loan balance:

$$\$105,000.00 - \$99.62 = \$104,900.38$$

These steps are repeated for 12 months to calculate the full year's breakdown between interest and principal. Table 2.1 shows a full calculation for the first two years based on the five steps above.

TABLE 2.1　Monthly Mortgage Payment Breakdown
6.25% 30-Year Amortization

Month	Payment	Interest	Principal	Balance
Balance				$105,000.00
1	$ 646.50	$ 546.88	$ 99.62	104,900.38
2	646.50	546.36	100.14	104,800.24
3	646.50	545.83	100.67	104,699.57
4	646.50	545.31	101.19	104,598.38
5	646.50	544.78	101.72	104,496.66
6	646.50	544.25	102.25	104,394.41
7	646.50	543.72	102.78	104,291.63
8	646.50	543.19	103.31	104,188.32
9	646.50	542.65	103.85	104,084.47
10	646.50	542.11	104.39	103,980.08
11	646.50	541.56	104.94	103,875.14
12	646.50	541.02	105.48	103,769.66
Total	$7,758.00	$6,527.66	$1,230.34	

Second Year

Month	Payment	Interest	Principal	Balance
Balance				$103,769.66
1	$ 646.50	$ 540.47	$ 106.03	103,663.63
2	646.50	539.91	106.59	103,557.04
3	646.50	539.36	107.14	103,449.90
4	646.50	538.80	107.70	103,342.20
5	646.50	538.24	108.26	103,233.94
6	646.50	537.68	108.82	103,125.12
7	646.50	537.11	109.39	103,015.73
8	646.50	536.54	109.96	102,905.77
9	646.50	535.97	110.53	102,795.24
10	646.50	535.39	111.11	102,684.13
11	646.50	534.81	111.69	102,572.44
12	646.50	534.23	112.27	102,460.17
Total	$7,758.00	$6,448.51	$1,309.49	

It is always important to check your math whenever performing calculations. In this case, there are two important quick checks. First, the total of interest and principal should be the same as the total of 12 months' payments. On the table for the first year:

$$\$6,527.66 + \$1,230.34 = \$7,758.00$$

The second verification involves a comparison from the loan balance at the beginning and end of the year. The difference should be the same as the total of principal payments. On the table:

$$\$105,000.00 - 103,769.66 = \$1,230.34$$

The second year's calculations also balance out in the same way. The purpose of this exercise is to isolate the principal and interest payments in order to calculate cash flow as accurately as possible. The one-year table is an example of loan *amortization* and this would continue for 30 years, at which time the balance would go to zero.

The details of interest and principal breakdown are important for the purpose of cash flow calculations, as demonstrated later in this chapter. If a lender provides this information for you, that is an advantage; but if you want to calculate it ahead of time—an essential exercise in controlling your cash flow—you will need to know how to break down the payments over the coming year.

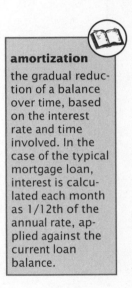

amortization
the gradual reduction of a balance over time, based on the interest rate and time involved. In the case of the typical mortgage loan, interest is calculated each month as 1/12th of the annual rate, applied against the current loan balance.

Rental Expense and Tax Calculations

Why is it essential to calculate your cash flow in advance? At the very least, you need to estimate the outcome of a full year's cash flow, to decide whether it makes sense to buy the property. A stock market investor considers dividend payments, revenue, and earnings, and looks at the price history of a stock to identify risk levels and to decide which stocks to buy. A real estate investor has to do the same thing.

An expensive myth is: All real estate is profitable and buying into real estate will make you rich. This is false. If you pick the *wrong* real estate or invest in a weak market, you are inviting disaster. The wrong market includes one in which the prices of average homes are too high to make positive cash flow, given market rents. The two markets—home value and rental demand—are separate and apart from one another. In the ideal market, home prices are relatively low, and likely to increase in the future, and rental demand is very strong. In the worst type of market for rental income property, real estate prices are high and rental demand is low. You need to estimate the mortgage payment you will need to make, and to identify the amount of market-rate rent you can expect to earn on a property, *before* you buy.

The calculation should include not just your mortgage payment, but all other expenses as well. It also should extend to figuring out your tax benefits, which means you have to also estimate depreciation (see Chapter 7). For the purpose of calculating after-tax cash flow, we are going to use a depreciation value without going into detail.

However, you will need to know how to estimate depreciation value of real estate as part of this calculation.

Here is an example that uses typical or average numbers:

House cost	$150,000
Down payment	$45,000
Mortgage payment	$646.50
First year principal	$1,230
First year interest	$6,528
Insurance	$465
Property taxes	$642
Utilities you will pay	$360

Depreciation is based on estimated breakdown of property valued as $30,000 for land and $120,000 for house (land cannot be depreciated). First-year depreciation will be one-half the annual total, so the calculated depreciation value is lower here than in future years, which will allow $4,364 per year in our example (see Chapter 7):

First-year	$2,182
Effective tax rate, federal and state combined	42%

We need to know this level of detail in order to figure the after-tax cash flow. Using this information and the worksheet in Table 2.2, we can estimate the first-year cash flow.

Depreciation is calculated over 27.5 years, but first-year depreciation is cut in half. (The reason is explained in Chapter 7.) Your *effective tax rate* is the percentage of your taxable income that will be due, given combined federal and state tax rates. For example, if your effective federal rate is 33 percent and the state rate is 9 percent, your total effective tax rate is 42 percent. So any additional income beyond what you will make at current levels will be taxed at 42 percent (and any reductions in income will reduce your tax liability by 42 percent).

The cash flow worksheet is revealing. It demonstrates that the first-year cash flow is $775 negative, but the second-year cash flow is $109 positive. This is due primarily to the differences in depreciation. The first-year deduction is one-half of the subsequent years. Depreciation is a noncash expense, so it provides value in the form of reduced tax liabilities, but it has no effect on cash flow. Note that the total of payment in both years is identical: Both are $9,225. This is because the differences in mortgage principal and interest are different in each year, however in total they add up to the same payment amount.

> **effective tax rate**
> the rate of taxes you pay, combining federal and state liabilities, based on income levels. The effective rate is the rate you will pay based on your current taxable income. Any additional income will be subject to tax at the effective rate and any reductions in taxable income will reduce tax liabilities by the same rate.

From this worksheet, you could conclude that your cash flow is slightly favorable by the second year, *assuming* no lapses in rent or unexpected repairs, and no increases in your estimates of other expenses. From this exercise, you could conclude that rental income has covered mortgage payments (including $2,539 in principal payments, which adds to your equity). There is a trade-off here. If we apply this analysis over many years, that trade-off is acceptance of investment risk, in exchange for ever-increasing equity. The risk of vacancies and unexpected repairs or maintenance, may be a worthwhile and acceptable risk. For example, you may limit the analysis of equity to the $2,539 in the example; but if property values are also rising on average by 5 percent per year, then your $150,000 has also increased in market value:

$$[1.05 \times 150,000]^2 = \$165,375$$

The average of 5 percent per year is a reasonable assumption in many areas. Remembering that all real estate markets are local, the use of any nationwide averages is going to be inaccurate; some areas will under-achieve and others will perform far better. But for purposes of illustration, we could look at this cash flow analysis as providing a net increase in investment value:

TABLE 2.2　After-Tax Cash Flow Calculation Worksheet

Description	First Year Annual Expense	First Year Annual Other Payment	Second Year Annual Expense	Second Year Annual Other Payment
Estimated rent income	$7,200		$7,200	
Mortgage payment:				
Principal		1,230		1,309
Interest	6,528		6,449	
Insurance	465		465	
Property taxes	642		642	
Utilities	360		360	
Total payments	7,995	1,230	7,916	1,309
Plus: Depreciation	2,182		4,364	
Total expenses	10,177		12,280	
Net profit or loss	−2,977		−5,080	
Tax effect, 42%	1,250		2,134	
After-tax cash flow:				
Total cash flow in:				
Rental income	$7,200		$7,200	
Tax benefits	1,250		2,134	
Total	$8,450		$9,334	
Total payments:				
Cash expenses	$7,995		$7,916	
Principal	1,230		1,309	
Total	$9,225		$9,225	
Net cash flow in or (−) out	$ −775		$ 109	

Year 1

Cash flow	−775
Equity from mortgage payments	1,230
Equity from growth in market value	7,500
First-year investment profit	7,955

Year 2

Cash flow	109
Equity from mortgage payments	1,309
Equity from growth in market value	<u>7,875</u>
Second-year investment profit	<u>9,293</u>
Total increase in investment value	<u>17,248</u>

We have to expand this analysis even further to accurately analyze cash flow and investment profits together. The growth in market value above is based on the initial value of the property, which was $150,000. However, referring back to our example, the original mortgage is $105,000 and you put $45,000 down. So if we want to accurately assess the investment value of your investment, we need to base these numbers on the amount you invested:

Year 1

Original investment, down payment	$45,000
First-year investment profit	7,955
Annual return	<u>17.7%</u>

Year 2

Basis of investment (original value plus annual return)	$52,955
Second-year investment profit	9,293
Annual return	<u>17.5%</u>

From this more accurate analysis, we develop a reliable means for comparing rental income property investing to other forms of investing. For example, would you be able to average more than 17 percent per year in the stock market? Most investors do not.

The side-to-side comparison between stocks and rental income investing is not reliable in every respect. This cash-flow based analysis is instructive because it demonstrates the hidden profits that are possible with rental income investing. However, the types and degrees of risk in the two investments are vastly different. For example, as shown in Table 2.3, there are numerous risk elements that make such comparisons less than reliable.

The value in comparing investment returns is that it provides a means for how you can best plan ahead. You probably do not want to put all of your investment capital in the stock market from now until retirement; you probably would hesitate to invest it all in real estate. Given the various risk levels and types of risk, there are positive and negative points to be made for either market.

TABLE 2.3 Risk Comparisons between Real Estate and Stocks	
Real Estate	*Stocks*
Investment is leveraged, so the cash flow risk exposure is substantial.	Investment is not necessarily leveraged, so there is no cash flow risk.
The property is insured so that a catastrophic loss will not threaten investment value.	Stocks cannot be insured, so a serious decline in market value can create serious losses.
The real estate market is illiquid; it is expensive to buy and sell property.	The stock market is highly liquid; it is easy and inexpensive to buy and sell.
Unit value of real estate is high.	Unit value of real estate is low.
Investors have direct, personal control over property and can increase market value through personal effort.	Stockholders have an equity position but no control over day-to-day operations of the company.

Even when your cash flow comes out extremely close, as in the preceding example, it may be worth holding the investment for the long term—as long as property values are rising. It is reasonable to say that rental income covers the total of all expenses and payments (again, assuming no surprises) and that, in the long term, you will benefit from market price appreciation over many years. When you add cash flow analysis to growth in investment value—based on your original cash investment—the outcome for real estate can be impressive. This has to be balanced against the various risks and compared objectively to the stock market or to simply placing cash in a savings account. All such decisions offer different profit potential as well as different risk profiles.

Tax Planning for Rental Income Property

The tax aspects of cash flow planning are easily overlooked; but they are substantial. In the detailed example earlier in this chapter, we used 42 percent as the effective tax rate. This is reasonable if we assume a 33 percent federal and 9 percent state tax rate. The cash flow impact of depreciation is most important because that expense (which is deductible but requires no cash outlay). Again referring to our example, the year-to-year cash benefit of depreciation is $1,833 ($4,364 × 42%), or about $153 per month.

This is not a lot of money. However, if you end up owning four or five rental income properties, and your investment level is higher per property than in our example, the combined monthly cash flow benefit can mean the difference between a smooth-working investment program and a financial struggle. The tax benefits are essential.

In assessing the practicality of rental income investments, you need to be aware of some tax essentials. Rental income investing is unique because it is the only type of investment in which losses are deductible at such a high level (you are allowed to deduct as much as $25,000 per year in net losses from rental income property activity). For example, if you report capital losses in stocks or mutual funds, you are limited to only $3,000 maximum deduction per year. If you invest in limited partnerships and similar "passive activity" investments (see Chapter 7), you are not allowed to deduct net losses at all. Those losses have to be carried over to future years and can be deducted only as offsetting deductions against other gains. So real estate investors enjoy a privileged status under the tax laws.

Depreciation is calculated on the value of improvements. So the building's value is subject to depreciation, but land itself cannot be depreciated. For residential property, the value is generally depreciated over 27.5 years. So in the example of improvements worth $120,000, the annual depreciation (except for the first year) is:

$$\$120,000 \div 27.5 = \$4,364$$

The maximum annual loss deduction in real estate is $25,000. If your losses exceed the amount you are allowed to deduct, the excess is carried over and applied to future years. However, if your adjusted gross income is more than $100,000, your maximum loss is reduced 50 cents for each dollar above that threshold. So if your adjusted gross income is $102,000, you are allowed a maximum real estate loss deduction of $24,000; and if your adjusted gross income is $110,000, your maximum real estate loss is $20,000:

	Example 1	Example 2
Adjusted gross income	$102,000	$110,000
Deductibility ceiling	−100,000	−100,000
Excess	$2,000	$10,000
Maximum annual deduction	$25,000	$25,000
One-half excess (above)	−1,000	−5,000
Maximum deductible	$24,000	$20,000

This topic is explained in more detail in Chapter 7. For the purpose of understanding the importance of cash flow, we need to consider a few points about taxes:

1. Tax benefits (especially regarding the deductibility of depreciation as a noncash expense) are essential elements in computing net cash flow.

2. Capital losses are limited to a maximum deduction per year of $3,000; however, in rental income investments, you can deduct up to $25,000 per year, a significant tax advantage.

3. If your adjusted gross income is more than $100,000 per year, the tax benefits of investing in rental income property are limited; above $150,000, no losses are deductible.

adjusted sales price

the price at which property is sold, minus all costs of sale. Costs include real estate commissions paid as well as all other seller expenses: recording fees, reconveyance, partial payments of utilities, interest and taxes; and expenses paid for improvements in anticipation of the sale.

Does the limitation of deductions for high-income investors make real estate impractical? No. In fact, there is an important difference between loss deductions and income shelter. In our example earlier in this chapter, we estimated annual rental income at $7,200 per year. That income will not be taxed as long as expenses meet or exceed that level. So the income from rents is tax-sheltered by deductible losses. However, any net loss calculated from rental income activity has to be carried over and applied against future years. Here, another potential benefit may arise. If you have highly profitable real estate activity a few years from now, profits will be sheltered by the accumulated loss carryover, reducing future tax liabilities. For example, when you sell rental income property, your total gain is reduced by any carryover loss you were unable to claim in prior years.

Another oddity in the tax law that requires planning—often years in advance—is the rule concerning sale of investment property. When you sell, your capital gain is computed as the net difference between the *adjusted sales price* (price minus real estate commissions and other costs) and *adjusted purchase price* of the property; and the gain is then increased by the sum of depreciation you deducted over the years. Reporting depreciation in this way is referred to as a *recapture* of those deductions.

An example of how capital gain is computed: If you originally purchase property for $150,000 and sell it eight years later for $250,000, it appears at first glance that the profit is $100,000. But further assume that your original purchase closing costs were $1,235 and your closing costs at sale were $17,450. We will also assume that you claimed $32,730 in depreciation. To expand this argument even further, we assume that your annual losses could not be fully deducted, and you have accumulated $12,400 in carryover losses. The computation of your capital gain, given these specifics, is:

Sales price	$250,000
Less: Closing costs paid	−17,450
Adjusted sales price	$232,550
Purchase price	$150,000
Plus: Closing costs paid	−1,235
Adjusted purchase price	$151,235
Gross profit	$81,315
Other adjustments:	
Depreciation recapture	32,730
Less: unused loss carryover	−12,400
Taxable capital gain	$101,645

adjusted purchase price
the original price at which property is purchased, plus all costs paid by the buyer to acquire the property. These costs include inspection fee, escrow, title insurance, legal fees paid, recording and documentation fees, and other expenses required to be paid by the buyer.

The maximum tax on long term capital gains is 15 percent. However, the recapture portion will be taxed as high as 25 percent and is not counted for the lower rate. This example ends up fairly close to the difference between purchase and sale prices; however, it consists of many segments. The longer you own property, the higher the depreciation recapture and the more likely the overall gain will be higher as well. So while this example makes little net difference, its various parts are important to consider.

The tax law provides a clue about another interesting preplanning point. Under today's rules, your personal residence—defined as a house you have used as your *primary residence* for at least two of the past five years—can be sold for as much as $500,000 profit, without any tax liability. This can occur any number of times without limit, but you cannot claim a primary residence deduction more often than once every two years.

recapture
a rule in the tax code requiring that the sum of all depreciation deducted while the property is owned, is to be added to the profit (or deducted from the loss) at the time the property is sold.

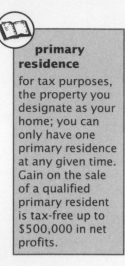

primary residence

for tax purposes, the property you designate as your home; you can only have one primary residence at any given time. Gain on the sale of a qualified primary resident is tax-free up to $500,000 in net profits.

This tax rule opens up some interesting advance planning possibilities. For example, what if you convert a rental property to your primary residence at least two years before you sell? Can you avoid tax on it? An investment property is taxed as a capital gain, but if you convert an investment property to your primary residence and live there at least two years, you can escape that tax. However, you would be taxed on depreciation recapture and you would not be allowed to deduct carryover losses. The majority of the gain would not be taxed, though, because it would quality under the primary residence rule.

Yet another tax advantage you enjoy is the ability to defer taxes on profits you earn when you exchange an investment property for another one. Generally, you have to buy a property that costs as much as the amount you get upon sale, and you have to complete the transaction within a time limited; but this exchange allows you to put off the tax liability until years later. Chapter 7 provides the details of these tax deferred exchanges.

These major points make it clear that as a rental income property investor, you need to (1) be aware of the special tax rules and benefits and (2) plan ahead, often for many years, to maximize your profits and minimize your tax liabilities.

In the next chapter, we learn about the potential of the fixer-upper market, one of the most profitable methods for investing in rental income property.

Fixer-Upper Alternatives
The Flipping Market

Entering the rental income property market the traditional way is to purchase a residential property and rent it out. This is obvious and straightforward—but it is not always the most profitable or the most practical way to go.

In some markets, slow demand or excess housing inventory impedes the desirable pace of growth in value. Every investor wants investment value to increase, and in comparison between investments, the faster-growing choices are always desirable as long as risks are acceptable within the same range. Some markets have a high demand for units, so market rents are attractive and vacancies are low. At the same time, it is possible that property values are flat and appear likely to remain so for the indefinite future. In these situations, you may seek a strategic approach to entering the market outside of the traditional channels.

This is where the *fixer-upper* enters the picture. By definition, such a property needs to contain four essential attributes:

1. It has to be priced below current market rates for similar homes, because improvements are needed.
2. The work required to be performed to bring the property up to average or better condition is minimal.
3. The time required for such improvements is not excessive.
4. The cost of improvements is less than the potential short-term increase in market value.

fixer-upper

a property priced below current market prices because work needs to be performed, which offers the potential for fast profits as long as repairs can be performed without great expense and in a short period of time.

The fixer-upper market is a short-term one. You maximize your profits when you are able to turn over these properties in as short a period of time as possible. The idea is not to benefit from long-term growth in value, but from the immediate improvements you perform specifically to bring a depressed property up to market standards.

The idea of buying low-priced properties, fixing them up, and selling at a profit, may seem like a no-brainer. However, the process could be a nightmare if you do not research the market and the specific property in advance. You need to know exactly what kinds of improvements will be required and what those improvements are going to cost. You also need to be able to compare the price of the property to average prices for similar homes, and to then decide whether the level of work will justify the risk. This equation has to include the cost of repairs as well as the expense of buying and selling the property; your skill level; and the time you need to spend working on the property.

The Flipping Concept

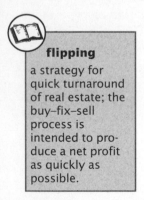

flipping

a strategy for quick turnaround of real estate; the buy–fix–sell process is intended to produce a net profit as quickly as possible.

When you buy a home in poor condition, fix it up and then sell it, the process is called *flipping*. It is descriptive. You buy, fix, and sell as quickly as possible; speed is essential because, unless you have the luxury of a lot of cash, the cost of owning the property includes either interest on a loan or the use of capital you could use elsewhere.

An important distinction should be made between flipping properties that are also fixer-uppers; and becoming involved in *distressed properties*. Some real estate experts buy properties at auction or in foreclosure or estate sales with the idea of finding a buyer immediately. In some situations, the buyer may be lined up in advance, so the transaction can take as little as a few hours. A distressed property is one available at a discount from its market value, due to the owner's financial or legal problems, or poor condition, or both.

The market for distressed properties is highly specialized and full of potential pitfalls and most beginners will be wise to gain quite a lot of experience before considering going into this market. It is often the case that properties are available at a discount for a good reason. Those reasons may also affect your ability to resell the property, so a lot of expertise is needed. Do not be drawn in by television and newspaper ads promising fast riches in real estate with no money down, the real estate government auction, or other similar but very exotic markets. The truth is that for most people, investing in rental income property, whether in perfect condition or a fixer-upper, requires careful research, investment capital, time and effort, and some personal risk. While all of these requirements are going to be found in any kind of investment, real estate in unique because *you* can largely determine the timing of profits, the degree and cost of work involved, and the types of properties in which you will invest.

distressed properties
real estate available at a discount due to an owner's financial problems or poor condition, which may be quickly flipped and sold at a profit.

So flipping properties brings in two markets that often are separate: fixer-uppers (generally, properties whose value is discounted due to condition) and flipped properties (those that are discounted either due to condition or an owner's financial problems). You can flip properties, often in a fairly short holding period, and earn a profit. Or in some circumstances, it could be desirable to hold onto the problem for longer than a few months, perhaps converting it to a rental property and holding it indefinitely. Conditions are going to dictate which approach will work best for you.

The profit potential in flipping properties can be considerable. It all depends on your ability to pick properties well. The *ideal* flip candidate is one where the owner wants to get out quickly (for whatever reasons), and when the condition of the property is poor. The needed work should be cosmetic. The two best forms of cosmetic repair are yard work and outside painting. So many well-constructed houses make a bad first impression simply because they look like a lot of work. You will find that cleaning up and landscaping a yard can be very fast and inexpensive; and painting a house is also going to add tremendously to the property's value, but does not require a great amount of skill. (In comparison, roofing, plumbing, electrical and structural problems can be very expensive and require highly specialized and expensive help.)

It is often the case that a current owner either does not realize the potential in such easy fixes, or simply does not care. The owner could hire someone to work on the property for two or three days and, for only a few hundred dollars, vastly improve market value. Some owners just want to sell right now. They may live out of the area and just do not know how to go about finding someone to do the work; or they might not understand the value of the cosmetic fix. If the local real estate market is slow, the fixer-upper is difficult to sell, especially if buyers are like those would-be sellers. Many buyers want to find properties that are perfect and require no work. A minority of buyers can look beyond the poor first impression, but most will reject houses that make a poor impression. This is where you have an advantage, especially is slower markets.

By locating those properties needing work, you can pick them up for prices below market value, often far below. A quick turnaround is possible for certain types of cosmetic repairs, and investing in specific types of improvements is likely to yield higher profits. By the same argument, some repairs do not add a lot to the value of the property, and are not worth the expense that is going to be involved. See Chapter 4 for a detailed comparison between different types of repairs and improvements.

Attributes of High-Potential Properties

Just as stock investors try to find stocks that are most likely to grow in value, real estate investors have to research their market. Many misconceptions, especially in strong markets, obscure the importance of research for picking properties intelligently. Among these misconceptions are:

1. In "hot" markets, it does not matter what you buy. Everything is moving up.

2. A real estate agent can show you good properties; you do not need to investigate.

3. You can afford to invest in properties even when you experience *negative cash flow* because ultimately you will make money.

negative cash flow
a situation in which rental income property investors have to pay more money out than they receive from rents.

These real estate myths cause a lot of trouble, especially among novice investors. It always matters what you buy because, even in very strong markets, there are always some properties that remain flat or even decline in value. Second, you cannot depend solely on an agent's advice—you have to take responsibility for investigating the attributes, value, and rental demand for a property, a neighborhood, and a region. Third, the idea that it is all right to buy property even when cash flow is negative can create financial havoc and make profits elusive and, in some cases, impossible.

Imagine a situation in which your mortgage payment is $250 per month higher than the rents you receive. You might even be able to afford to pay that extra $250. But what happens if you have a three-month vacancy? Unexpected repairs? A tenant who stops paying rent? Increases in utilities, property taxes, insurance, or interest in a variable-rate mortgage? Any of these conditions will increase that negative cash flow. Furthermore, each time you have to pay money into maintaining the investment, it erodes your paper profits, making it more difficult to sell at a profit later. For example, if your investment property's value is growing by about $5,000 per year, negative cash flow of $250 per month eats up 60 percent of your paper profits; and any unexpected additional drains on cash may quickly absorb the rest. It is ill-advised to intentionally accept negative cash flow, even if you are told the market is hot.

Attributes of good fixer-upper candidates include features such as:

1. *Strong current market demand.* Just as a stock market investor spends time studying the attributes of the stock and the company, real estate investors need to understand their market. In your study of real estate, you will want to be aware of the three markets: for properties, rentals, and financing. If you are planning to invest in fixer-upper properties in areas dominated by owner-occupied houses, for example, you may want to look for properties with the greatest promise for short-term growth in market value. Specifically, such houses should be available at a discount because of the need for cosmetic repairs, and the premise for flipping such properties is based on the idea that they can be quickly brought up to market rates. If you intend to sell the property as a rental or to keep it and convert it to a rental, you will be equally interested in the local market demand for rental units. The strength of the local housing market is not a dependable measurement of such demand, because it is a separate market with its own supply and demand attributes. Converting a fixer-upper to a rental is a variation on the flipping theme and the strategic possibilities are explained in more detail in Chapter 5.

2. *Specific range of improvements required.* In reviewing potential properties for flipping, you will need to be aware of the specific types of improvements needed. This is a technical point and may require help from an inspector or contractor. The next chapter identifies types of improvements and how to classify them. If you are knowledgeable about repairs and renovations yourself, that is a valuable talent in the fixer-upper market. If you are not, it is equally valuable to have a contractor available to advise you about which properties will be the best candidates for fixer-upper and flipping.

3. *Desirable neighborhood features.* With emphasis on the condition of a specific house, it is easy to overlook the equally important neighborhood features. At times, various neighborhoods go through transitions and these times present buying opportunities—assuming the transition is a positive one (families buying homes, older homes being improved, low crime rates, pride of ownership). If the transition is negative (empty lots, poor landscaping and repairs, increasing crime levels, rentals left empty for many months) then the area is not going to have

good potential for you. Some specialists seek the negative transition neighborhood to find distressed properties based on the premise that these can be bought and flipped for a fast profit. However, while this market exists, it is better left to experienced real estate speculators; this is not a market for first-time novice investors.

4. *Strong construction features.* The types of repairs you can see—the need for new paint, landscaping, or a roof—are only one classification that defines condition of a property. You will want to seek houses that are well built, including structural features not visible to the naked eye. The invisible areas, including the internal systems, are where potential problems may lie, and these could also be very expensive to fix; so you need to have an expert advise you, either your own contractor or a professional and independent inspector. One serious risk in the fixer-upper market is assuming that the visible repairs are all that is needed, only to discover that far more serious and expensive problems exist as well. In such cases, it could be impossible to get out of the investment at a profit.

bridge loan
a form of financing granted during construction or, for fixer-upper properties, for a limited number of months during which repairs are completed. Interest accumulates during the bridge period, but no payments are required until the bridge period has expired.

gap financing
a form of financing designed for developers, builders, and investors in fixer-upper properties. A limited time period in which no payments are required, enables fixer-upper investors to complete repairs without concern for cash flow, with the loan and interest payable at the end of the period.

5. *Desirable financing terms.* The reason a lot of properties are flipped as quickly as possible is that financing presents a problem. The longer the period required for making periodic mortgage payments, the more your profits are eroded. Ideally, if you plan to sell the property, you need to complete repair and sell as fast as possible. One alternative is to fix the property and rent it out, so that rental income will pay the mortgage; this gives you flexibility in deciding when to sell. For example, you might prefer to wait until the start of the selling season. In most regions, this is spring to summer. So if you complete your repairs in the early fall, it may be difficult to find a buyer. You may also be able to find some form of *bridge loan*, a type of financing often used during construction of new properties. This is also called *gap financing* because it is granted for a limited period of time, usually only a few months. While no payments are required during the bridge period, interest accumulates and is payable when the limited period expires.

Quick Fix versus Expensive Problems

Most fixer-upper investors want to find very good bargains in properties that look terrible, but need only fast, inexpensive cosmetic repairs. So getting rid of overgrown weeds in the yard and doing some basic landscaping, painting the house, and repairing minor damage, are examples of the best possible fixer-upper properties. These are also examples of the kinds of repairs that can be done quickly; if you want to flip properties you find in a state of disrepair, these quick fix solutions can maximize your profits.

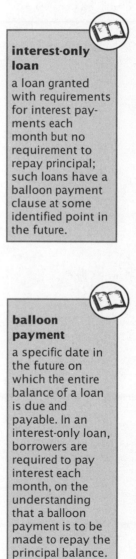

interest-only loan
a loan granted with requirements for interest payments each month but no requirement to repay principal; such loans have a balloon payment clause at some identified point in the future.

The time required to complete repairs is an essential element of the equation. The longer the period you own the property, the more you have to pay in interest. The interest-only portion of a mortgage obligation is substantial. Even if you have a bridge loan, the interest accumulates, so a holding period should be as short as possible. For example, if you borrow $100,000 and your loan is granted at 6.25 percent, your first month's interest will be $521 (based on a 30-year amortization schedule). If your loan is an *interest-only loan*, you are obligated for that amount each and every month, as well as for the principal. This interest obligation reduces your potential profit, so the longer you own the property, the lower your profits. With an interest-only loan, you want to sell the property as soon as possible. At the very least, you will want to either rewrite the loan (if you decide to convert the property to a rental and hold onto it) or sell before the *balloon payment* comes due.

balloon payment
a specific date in the future on which the entire balance of a loan is due and payable. In an interest-only loan, borrowers are required to pay interest each month, on the understanding that a balloon payment is to be made to repay the principal balance.

One risk of going into the flipping market is that you may not be able to sell when you intend to. Repairs may take longer than you thought or you may discover additional problems you did not anticipate. Or, in the worst outcome of all, you may be unable to find a buyer at the price you need in order to make a profit, or even to break even on the venture.

With time as the essential ingredient in this form of investing, you need to be very thorough in your evaluation of properties and also of the market itself. If the market is slow, meaning few buyers are on the scene, it does not matter how nicely you fix up the property. If there is little or no demand, it is going to take time to complete a sale. If you intend to convert the property to a rental, you also have to ensure that there is adequate demand for rental units and that market rents are adequate to cover your mortgage obligation. If you have negotiated a bridge loan or an interest-only loan, you also need to en-sure—in advance—that you will have alternatives. The current lender or a new one will have to be available to write a permanent loan for your newly acquired rental property if you are unable to sell.

If you are not a skilled contractor, you will probably want to avoid buying homes with expensive problems. Your profit margin can be quickly eroded and even surpassed if you need to repair structural problems or replace plumbing, electrical, or heating systems in the house. The worst outcome is one in which the property is "totaled" because the cost of needed repairs exceeds the equity in the property. For example, if you buy a fixer-upper for $80,000 and put down $24,000, you may hope that you can bring market value up to $100,000 at a cost of about $5,000:

Target market value, net of sales expenses	$100,000
Less: Cost of the property	$80,000
Less: Cost of repairs	5,000
Total costs	$85,000
Potential equity profit	$15,000

This basic calculation gives you some guidance as to what you can and should expect from the fixer-upper venture. You plan to flip the property within three months, for example, so your interest cost *should* reduce your equity profit by about $1,500. This requires that you complete repairs, list the property, and complete the sale, all within three months, a very fast-track schedule. It is diffi-cult to imagine completing a flip more quickly. However, what if you discover after purchasing the property that there is an additional $20,000 of damage that has to be fixed? In this situation, there is no way to earn back your invest-ment or to make a profit. The only way to escape the transaction is to lose money. This means you will have to convert the property to a rental and wait out the market. This is a most undesirable situation because it means you have no real equity. Unless you can find someone to buy the property at your target price, even with the expensive flaws unfixed, you are stuck with a loss.

The conversion to rental, when you would rather flip the property, is an undesirable outcome. You cannot simply walk away from the obligation and let the lender foreclose. That would affect your credit badly and prevent you from getting future loans for real estate investments and for other reasons. It could have other consequences as well, such as preventing you from being able to refi-nance existing home equity loans, cancellation of credit cards or lines of credit, and a long-term bad mark on your credit score.

You are better off avoiding the problem of hidden flaws *before* buying property.

Importance of Home Inspections

The best way to avoid expensive problems is by paying for a professional home inspection. This costs money, of course. You cannot afford to order a home inspection for every property you look at, so you should limit the expense to only those properties you are considering very seriously. The cost is going to vary by region, size of the property, and age. If the property has a septic system or well, additional types of testing may be required, compared to properties on local water and sewer service.

A good place to begin is on the Web site of the American Society of Home Inspectors (see Valuable Resource) where you can locate names, addresses and phone numbers of local inspectors licensed by ASHI. It is crucial to use an inspector who is qualified, professional, and free from conflicts of interest. For example, it is not wise to hire a contractor to perform a home inspection if the same person offers to fix any discovered problems. You need a completely objective inspector in order to get an honest, complete report.

The ASHI has been testing and qualifying professional home inspectors for many years. The procedures are designed to prevent conflict of interest situations. For example, an ASHI member agrees to live with a Code of Ethics. This code forbids inspectors from doing inspections on any properties in which they have a financial interest; in any situation in which payment is based on future referrals; or when the inspector will refer you to someone else to perform repairs. The inspector also cannot offer to perform repairs following issue of the inspection report.

The ASHI inspectors also cannot accept any payments for making recommendations to contractors, real estate agents, attorneys, escrow companies and other resources. The report is to be prepared in writing and given only to the

---

Valuable Resource

Go to the ASHI Web site at http://www.ashi.org/ to (1) find inspectors near you or (2) to check on the credentials of someone in your area who claims to be an ASHI member in good standing. The more verification you perform, the better.

individual paying for the service. If the report is to be shown to anyone else, such as a lender or seller, the person paying for the service has to give the inspector permission in advance. (An exception exists: If an immediate dangerous hazard is discovered, the inspector should advise current owners or occupants immediately.)

The standard inspection includes a visual examination of the property, including heating systems, plumbing and electrical systems, visible insulation, internal walls, ceilings and floors, foundation, basement or garage, foundation, roof, and other structural conditions. The inspector issues a written report and presents it to you, which should include specific recommendations for areas needing to be fixed. From the point of view of responsibility for flaws, the real value of a written report is twofold. First, it discloses any flaws that might not be visible, so you will know in advance what will need attention. Second, if you later discover flaws not listed on the inspector's report, you may have legal recourse against the inspector for failing to do a thorough inspection. So every inspector, knowing they expose themselves to legal trouble for poor work, has the incentive to produce thorough and detailed work.

Another reason to use a professional inspector is due to their experience. A contractor may be just as qualified by virtue of job skills and experience, but will also have a conflict of interest. If the contractor is planning to fix any problems discovered during the inspection, it will not be completely objective. An ASHI inspector is not certified until he or she passes two technical exams *and* performs a minimum of 250 hours of home inspections. They also have to keep up their skills with annual continuation education time.

You may need additional inspections, depending on the area where the property is located. A pest inspection (called a *termite inspection* in the southern regions) is essential in order to discover whether any infestation exists or, at the very least, if conditions would invite future infestation. The pest inspection is normally separate from the home inspection and requires a different level of expertise. In fact, in many states, home inspectors are specifically banned from including pest inspection as part of their report. If they discover infestation, they may refer you to a pest inspection company and encourage you to get that separate report as well. The pest inspection will cost much less than the more comprehensive home inspection. Both are necessary.

If the property is on a septic system, it should also be inspected. If a home inspector is not qualified, you may need to hire an expert to ensure that the current septic is up to required standards and it in good working order. If the property has a well and water association membership, you may also need to test water to ensure it is potable and that there is an adequate supply.

The entire range of possible inspection work depends on the type of system, local rules and regulations, and condition, age, and location of the property. You may need to call for a number of special inspections and the costs could be significant. One solution is to negotiate for inspections as part of your offer on a property. For example, you could add a *contingency* to your contract specifying that the seller will pay for pest, water, and septic inspections; and the buyer will pay for a home inspection. You may also wish to elaborate. If any of those inspections turn up defects that have to be fixed, you could include a further contingency that the seller will agree to pay for all repairs.

Estimating Time and Cost Features

Entering the fixer-upper market and flipping properties in a timely manner defines the level of profitability that you will achieve. Because time equals interest costs, it is essential that you control that element, ensure that you buy and sell on your timetable, and that you find the best possible financing terms. This requires considerable skill. How do you estimate time requirements for fixing up a property and then placing it for sale? How long will it take to find a buyer and close the deal? With so many variables, your experience and skill in this submarket of real estate will determine how successfully you achieve your goals. Here are some suggested guidelines:

> **contingency**
> a clause in a real estate offer providing performance in the event that certain events occur or do not occur. Payment for inspections is a common example, and contingency clauses can further specify responsibility to pay for repairs, contingencies related to obtaining financing, selling other property, or other forms of performance by the buyer or by the seller, including deadlines for completion.

1. *Get estimates of contractor time, and then double.* You will succeed in flipping properties when you work with competent people. If you have a contractor or handyperson helping you, make sure they have the time to give your work top priority; if they cannot, then you are not going to be able to control your schedule. Even with the best help, insist on an estimate of the time required to complete all work they will perform. Then double that estimate to arrive at a reasonable time requirement.

2. *Also double cost estimates.* Both time and cost are difficult to pin down. But you can count on both running over estimates. This is not just pessimistic; it is realistic. To get a good sense of how long repairs will take and what they are going to cost, double it up.

3. *Identify work you can complete yourself—and make a schedule.* The highest profit margin will occur in work you do yourself. For most beginners, the purely cosmetic fixer-upper is easiest to work on and also easiest to flip at a profit and in a short time period. If you have limited

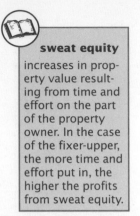

sweat equity
increases in property value resulting from time and effort on the part of the property owner. In the case of the fixer-upper, the more time and effort put in, the higher the profits from sweat equity.

carpentry skills, you can still perform your own painting and yard work, and save a lot by putting *sweat equity* into the deal.

4. *Estimate two months to list property for sale and close the deal.* Once you are ready to place property on the market for sale, you have to estimate the time required to find a buyer. In the best of markets it is safe to assume you will need two months. Once properties are listed, it takes time for the listing to filter down to the entire market, so two months is a reasonable allowance. Considering it may take approximately one month for a deal to close, even after the buyer and seller have come to an agreement, is also being realistic. In some very hot markets, you may get an offer on the first day you list the property . . . but do not count on it.

5. *List the property when your improvement deadline is within sight. Do not wait for completion.* If you know your improvements are going to be finished in the next few weeks, do not wait to list the property. Put it on the market today. Even if sellers view the property before repairs are completed, the progress of your work will be visible. Many buyers understand that work in progress is going to be completed by the time a deal closes. It does not make sense to wait until all of your improvements are done before listing the property.

6. *Find a real estate agent who aggressively markets your property.* It can be frustrating to work with a real estate agent who simply puts up a sign and does nothing more. You need an aggressive agent who will chase down buyers in many ways: holding open houses, listing the property prominently in local newspapers and magazines and on TV if a listing show is available in your area, working on commission incentive plans with other agents in the same firm. If your agent just puts up a "for sale" sign and never takes further action, you are not being well served. Find an aggressive agent before you enter a deal. Ask other property owners for referrals, and work only with those who close deals on a high volume.

7. *Work with a lender who can get you the best deals.* Finding a bridge loan at the best possible rates is also essential to your success. There are a few alternatives, but you need to shop around and make sure you get the best possible deal. This means finding the lowest rates and minimum costs. If you cannot find a competitive bridge loan in your area, consider using a *home equity line of credit* to finance your own flipping activities. Many consider this high risk because it involves using your

home equity and placing it at risk. However, if you are willing to take that level of risk, it could be the most inexpensive way to finance fixer-upper flipping. The reason: accessing home equity line of credit funds once the line is approved does not involve closing costs; you simply write a check against the line of credit.

8. *Coordinate* all *of the elements: cost, time, and financing.* Remember, the three elements of your flipping strategy have to be coordinated. It is a common mistake to think about these elements separately. First you find a property, estimate the time and cost to fix it up, and then figure out the financing plan. This is dangerous for a number of reasons. The time and cost elements may make the venture less than feasible, because interest expenses will absorb most or all of the profits; interest cost cannot be ignored in the equation. In fact, the estimate of costs should include monthly interest for the level of debt you will need to take on while you own the property.

> **home equity line of credit**
> financing based on the equity in your home. A lender grants the borrower a line of credit up to a specific level determined by the level of equity, and that line is used by writing a check, and repaid at monthly payment minimums or upon the sale of a fixer-upper, in a lump sum. The line can be used repeatedly.

Rental Income during Your Hold Period

Another aspect of flipping properties worth considering is that of rental income. Most people realize that one approach is to buy and fix up properties and then keep those properties as rentals, setting it up so that tenants produce cash flow to fund mortgage payments. That is the traditional method and if you can buy discounted properties, it also provides the greatest potential for cash flow. But you may also consider placing tenants in the property while repairs are being completed.

This is a high-risk suggestion. Even tenants who insist they will not mind having you and your contractor around, making noise and dust, and coming and going at all hours, are likely to become irritated once they actually move in. Time and again, novice investors tell tenant applicants that they are offering below-market rent *because* they will be repairing the property. It is human nature on the part of tenants to understand this at the time they apply, but to quickly forget it once they are in the property. Accept the fact that if you place tenants in your house while you are completing repairs, you could have conflict with them.

Some recommendations to overcome this potential problem follow:

1. *Document the terms of the agreement.* Set down exactly what you expect from the tenant in your rental contract. If part of the deal is that you will be coming and going, entering the property, and performing repairs on a daily basis, incorporate required advance notification into the deal. In every state, you are required to notify tenants before entering the property. (The rules often require 24 hours, for example.) As part of your original agreement, specify that you are giving the tenant perpetual 24-hour notice, and the tenant agrees.

2. *If practical, coordinate your work schedule with the tenant's schedule.* If your contractor has flexibility in when work is performed, coordinate that with the tenant. For example, if the tenant has children and the school schedule is hectic until 9 A.M. each weekday, have your work begin after 9 A.M. If tenants are gone all day at work, perform your repairs during those hours, and agree to close up for the day before they get home.

3. *Make sure your contractor always secures the property.* When you or your contractor leave the premises at times the tenant is not there, be sure you lock doors and windows and clean up any mess created that day. A tenant is going to become rightfully angry when they come home to unlocked doors and a big mess. Even though the disruptive nature of work in process is chaotic, you need to minimize the impact on the tenant, and to lock doors when you leave. If you or your contractor will be using the tenant's electricity, the actual percentage will be very low; even so, offer to pay a portion of the tenant's electrical bill or specify in your contract that rent is at its level in recognition that some utility cost will be yours.

4. *Set rent levels with the inconvenience factor in mind.* The rent you charge should be set well below market rates in exchange for access and inconvenience. This should be spelled out in your agreement. Remember, once the tenant gets used to paying rent at contracted levels, they are likely to forget that they are getting a discount.

5. *Specify that rent will increase once work is completed.* If you plan to allow the tenant to remain in the property when work has been completed, include in your contract the amount of additional rent you will charge. Also specify the date that increase is going to go into effect.

6. *If you are planning to put the property on the market, put that fact in the agreement and also specify terms for showing the property.* One of the greatest difficulties involving tenants arises when you are trying to sell the property. If a sale goes through, they may be given notice; so some

tenants will be uncooperative in your marketing efforts. Spell out conditions in your rental agreement concerning how and when real estate agents can show the property. Also recognize that agents often do not follow the rules unless they are given firm guidelines. For example, if your agreement is that tenants will always be given 24 hours' notice before property is shown, enforce that rule. Tell the tenant that if real estate agents show up with clients without making an appointment (and this *will* happen, perhaps frequently) the tenant has the right to refuse access to them. The appointment is necessary to maintain goodwill with the tenant.

7. *Enter into a month-to-month agreement.* You should always enter a month-to-month agreement when you are planning to flip property, especially if you are going to perform repairs and place the property on the market. You certainly do not want to be tied in to a long-term lease in these conditions. If tenants do not allow you access to make repairs, you will have unending conflict with them. In those conditions, a month-to-month rental agreement gives you the freedom to give notice and get unreasonable tenants out of the property.

8. *Give notice if the arrangement does not work out.* Whenever the arrangement does not work out, give notice to the tenants. You need to be in control. As long as you make every effort to respect the tenant's schedule and privacy, you have the right to expect cooperation in return. When that does not happen, you will be fighting an uphill battle until your final sale has been completed; and a disgruntled tenant may also try to sabotage a sale through hostility to real estate agents and potential buyers. Those conditions are not tolerable.

9. *Schedule repairs to minimize disruption to your tenants.* If you are performing repairs inside *and* outside, get the inside repairs out of the way as quickly as possible. It is less disruptive to tenants if you can perform work without needing to enter the property. For example, you can paint inside rooms and repair walls or floors before renting out the property. The outside work—landscaping, painting, roof repairs, for example—can take place after the tenant moves in. This makes it easier to maintain a positive relationship with the tenant.

10. *Be aware of state law when you enter this agreement.* No matter what your agreement states with the tenant, state law prevails and cannot be overruled with a contract. For example, you might get a tenant to agree to provide you access without 24 hours' notice; but if state law says you must provide such notice, your contract cannot be enforced. The agreement is intended to be cooperative: The tenant lets you have access when you need it, in exchange for a break on the rent. But if the tenant decides

after moving in that you have to follow the letter of the law, raise the rent or give them notice. You have the right in a month-to-month agreement to modify the terms and conditions. If you understand that your agreement may be overridden by the landlord-tenant rules, the tenant should also understand that you can give notice or raise rent when you choose.

In the best possible arrangement, a mature and intelligent tenant will happily accept a discount on the rent for the inconvenience of having you and your workers on site and, perhaps, coming in and out of the property. An inflexible tenant, one who wants the discount but does not want to uphold his or her end of the bargain, will impede your work and get in your way at every turn. You are better off speeding up the flip and having no tenant. But if you set up the deal so that everyone benefits, and if you take every possible step to minimize disruptions, you can have the best of both worlds: finding a good bargain on a fixer-upper, working with a cooperative tenant who has a discounted rent deal, and, eventually, either flipping the property at a good profit or converting it to a permanent rental with strong positive cash flow.

The next chapter explores the flipped property and its financial attributes in more detail: appearance and cosmetic repairs, classifications of repairs and their potential for return on your investment, and the impression your property makes on potential buyers.

4

The Fixer-Upper Property

Abused Homes with Potential

You would not want to buy *any* property on the theory that a fresh coat of paint will double its value. Just as careful and thorough research helps making profits in the stock market, the same is true in rental income property. The belief that, in a strong market, you can buy anything and make money is a dangerous fallacy.

In any kind of market, the attributes of fixer-uppers offering the greatest potential can be identified, their repair time and cost estimated, and location narrowed down. Whenever you start researching the market and find dozens of apparent bargains, something is wrong. You need to reduce the field. Ask yourself: If there are so many bargains, why has not someone else already taken them? By the process of elimination, you can reduce those dozens of potential fixer-upper properties down to a stronger, more logical handful. And by recognizing which repairs are going to add the most value for the least cost, you can also ensure that your fixer-upper venture will remain under your control and produce acceptable profits rather than expensive surprises.

Attributes of Fixer-Uppers

Among the important attributes of the fixer-upper is a gap between its available price and the average market prices of similar homes. For example, if you are reviewing three-bedroom, two-bath single-family homes in a defined neighborhood, what is the average sales price for such properties over the past year? And what is the price of the property you are considering?

Also check the typical closing costs for buying and selling property. In our examples, assume that you will pay 10 percent total closing costs in a real estate transaction. For purposes of estimating overall closing costs, we use 10 percent of sales price in examples. In some areas, this may be more. In some property deals, it can also vary due to the cost of inspections and other costs unique to that property. The most expensive closing costs will be a sales commission, which we average at 6 percent; title insurance costs; legal and escrow fees; and recording and document fees. If you have to pay points to a lender, inspection fees, or excise tax on the sale of real estate, your closing costs may be higher.

Look at an example: In one city, average properties in one neighborhood sell for $107,000. You are looking at three possible fixer-upper properties, all of which are available below that level. The asking prices for these properties are $91,950; $88,000; and $86,500. Also assume that your budget for fixing up these properties is limited to cosmetics: painting, landscaping, and some limited internal renovations, all totaling $5,000. A side-by-side comparison given these facts is presented in Table 4.1.

TABLE 4.1   Estimated Returns for Three Fixer-Upper Properties

	Property 1	Property 2	Property 3
Average sales price	$107,000	$107,000	$107,000
Estimated closing costs	− 10,700	− 10,700	− 10,700
Net	96,300	96,300	96,300
Average price	$ 91,950	$ 88,000	$ 86,500
Plus improvements	5,000	5,000	5,000
Total	$ 96,950	$ 93,000	$ 91,500
Net profit (loss)	$ (650)	$ 3,300	$ 4,800

There would be no point in pursuing the first property, since the estimate places you in a loss position. Although these are only estimates, you have to go with what your numbers tell you. On a comparative basis, it appears that the second and third properties hold more potential.

Among our assumptions, we have to believe that the cost of improvements is going to be approximately the same for all three of the properties being analyzed. If that is true, then the analysis has to proceed with more assumptions in mind. For example, based on variables such as the specific neighborhood, age and condition of the property, and other market considerations, you may actually believe that the first property has the best potential for growth in market value. So you may review the three properties on a series of possible assumptions, such as:

Assumption 1: *Once improved the property will be held for one to two years and rented out.* In this situation, the market potential and cash flow possibilities may be more important than the fast turnaround profit potential. If the rental demand is strong in your area, you may be able to achieve strong positive cash flow in any (or all) of these properties. So the question comes down to one of whether you want to proceed speculating on the fix-and-sell approach, or to convert a property acquired at a discount, into a longer-term investment.

Assumption 2: *The goal is going to be to complete repairs and sell property as fast as possible.* If you clearly want to turn the investment around as fast as possible, you will be drawn to property number three, which has the greatest potential for dollar return. This assumes, again, that the cost of improvements and the holding period of property are going to be similar and truly comparable for all three properties. To come to that conclusion, you need to ensure that market and neighborhood conditions of these three properties are similar.

Assumption 3: *The decision to keep property as a rental or to flip it as soon as possible will depend on actual repair costs and market conditions.* This assumption is based on the realization that many things can change. For example, actual improvement costs may be higher or lower than original estimates; your holding period might vary as well. Or the market, either for property or for rentals, can change during the time you own the property.

To demonstrate how conditions can affect your assumptions, consider the two examples that follow:

Example 1: A Changed Market. You purchased a property three months ago for $88,000 and have invested $5,000 in improvements. At the time you bought the property, comparable homes in the area were selling for an average of $107,000. Today, however, the market has changed considerably. Two months ago, the largest employer in town closed its doors and moved, putting many people out of work. As a consequence, many more properties are on the market and prices have declined. You cannot get $107,000 for the property, so you have decided to wait out the slow economic cycle, and convert the property to a rental.

Example 2: Unforeseen Good Fortune. You closed on a property last week that you bought for $86,500. Yesterday you were preparing the outside of the house for painting, while two helpers were removing brush from the yard. While you were working, someone showed up and made you an offer on the property, of $105,000. Because this would be a private sale, you would not need to pay a real estate commission, so your margin would be substantial. You doubt that you could make such an impressive profit by completing repairs. The potential buyer just wants you to finish the brush clearing and painting, and wants a fast close. He has been looking for property in this neighborhood, and likes the house, and does not care how much it cost you or how recently you closed on the deal.

These examples may represent extremes. You certainly cannot count on markets to remain the same and drastic change is possible. You cannot expect the elusive cash buyer to simply show up and offer you a substantial profit either; but these events do occur. This demonstrates that your well considered plans may be changed by the markets, or by unanticipated surprises, either positive or negative.

The Importance of Appearance

The numbers have to work. With any form of investing, this is always the case. Careful advance analysis is the best way to prevent mistakes in the selection of one property over another, and the numbers are a starting point. However, even before you get to the number crunching stage, what is the initial impression of the property?

The initial impression should be analyzed in two ways. First, if the house makes a horrible first impression because it is cosmetically depreciated, there is great potential. By making a few repairs, such properties can be fixed and transformed so that the first impression is far better. A second possibility, however, is more serious and cannot be fixed cosmetically. For example, assume that in a particular neighborhood, most houses are 2,500 square feet with double-car garages, three bedrooms and two baths, and modern kitchens on 10,000 square foot lots. One house is many years out of date. It is a one-bedroom, one-bath house with only 1,100 square feet of space; the kitchen is outdated and the lot is 5,000 square feet. In this situation, no amount of cosmetic repair can bring the house into line with other houses on the same block.

The lack of *conformity* to this property makes it a problem beyond fixer-upper classification. Houses that do not conform to the "typical" houses in the same area tend to suffer market value as a consequence. A house that is less than others (in terms of building and lot size, features, and age) will certainly be valued well below typical prices. The conformity problem works in the other direction as well. For example, a five-bedroom, three-bath home on a double lot in a neighborhood of three-bedroom, two-bath homes on single lots, is not likely to return the same rate of market value as the conforming properties.

conformity
a principle in real estate observing that housing values of similar properties tend to move in the same direction and at the same rate; and that homes with dissimilar features and attributes do not appreciate in value in the same way.

When houses have less than the typical house in the area, they do not conform. So an attempt to treat such a house as a fixer-upper may not yield market value you may expect. If the house conformed in terms of size, age, and attributes, you would have a reasonable basis to believe that you would be able to bring value up to neighborhood averages.

This works in reverse as well. Using the previous neighborhood example of a three-bedroom, two-bath house again, what would occur if a custom house were built that exceeded the conformity level? If typical prices are $107,000 and the custom house was built at a cost of $175,000, would its market value be $175,000? Probably not. Under the principle of conformity, the owner would lose some of that value because the house did not conform with typical houses in the neighborhood.

The appearance of a property is your first clue concerning conformity. As a critical judge of value, your initial impression tells you whether a particular house conforms or not. A house that is smaller, older, and that has less attributes is not likely to gain market value comparable to other properties; this is a different matter than a comparable property that *does* conform to its neighboring houses, but has fallen into disrepair. For the purpose of buying fixer-uppers and either flipping them or holding them for rental income, the rule should be that you restrict your search to prospective properties that conform to other properties in the same neighborhood.

The appearance of a house is your first hint about conformity. If you develop a critical eye, you can discern between cosmetic conforming properties and nonconforming properties in the area.

Recognizing Market Potential: Valuation Theories

Conformity is the first principle that determines potential for changes in market value. The nonconforming property—whether less or more than its neighbors—is problematical. Buyers tend to shy away from nonconforming properties, and for good reason. You can recognize market potential by being aware of conformity as well as through other means.

Five additional principles of valuation will help you to understand *why* properties gain or lose market value, and why comparisons between properties may not always be simple or straightforward. These five principles of valuation are:

1. The *principle of progression* is used in appraisals. It is an observation that lower-priced real estate has the potential for increase in value due to its proximity to higher-priced or higher-quality properties. On the basis of reviewing residential properties, for example, the advice may be offered to "buy the worst house on a good block." But progression means much more. Low-priced neighborhoods that are surrounded by higher-priced neighborhoods have the potential to grow in value due to their proximity. This is seen in suburbs based on proximity to higher-priced areas. The shorter the commute distance, the higher the values; so as closer areas fill up and property values grow, there is a tendency for the appreciation trend to move to the next area. People may be willing to commute 45 minutes at one price range, but may accept a 60-minute commute if they can pay less for properties located 15 minutes farther away from the city. Under the principle of progression, the lower-priced properties are likely to grow in value based on price trends in the next neighborhood or city. In comparison, a similar property located in a remote rural area will not experience the same influences on value.

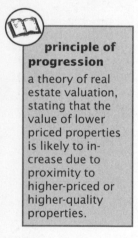

principle of progression

a theory of real estate valuation, stating that the value of lower priced properties is likely to increase due to proximity to higher-priced or higher-quality properties.

2. A similar theory of valuation is the *principle of regression*. This theory is the opposite of the principle of progression. Also used by appraisers, it is the observation that high-value real estate may be reduced or held back due to proximity to lower-value properties. Not only does conformity enter the equation; the mere fact that the next neighborhood (or town) over has lower-priced properties of comparable size and attributes, can prevent higher-priced properties from realizing their full potential. For the fixer-upper investor, this principle should be kept in

mind; there may be instances in which your comparison between asked price and "typical" market value will be limited by the principle of regression. If lower-priced properties are available nearby, your analysis may need to be adjusted for the limitation presented by the price disparity.

3. Another theory of valuation is called *highest and best use*. This theory states that property is going to be of maximum value when utilized in the best possible way. For example, property in a commercially zoned area that is used as a residence may not be valued the same as similar properties. Its highest and best use would be as a commercial space. When property is not used at its highest and best use, it will tend to bring less value than comparable properties. So on a street fronting a highway, dominated by small shops, a single-family residence is out of place and may not command the same price as similar residences a block or two away.

4. The whole structure of pricing is based on availability of properties suitable for a particular purpose. So the theory of *substitution* is important in the evaluation of property values. This theory states that when two similar properties are for sale, the lower-priced one will probably sell first. Furthermore, that price is likely to affect the sales price of the other property. This is an important observation for fixer-upper investing. For example, if typical prices in one area are $107,000 and you can buy a depreciated property for $86,500, the theory of substitution can work to your advantage. If your repairs bring that property up to neighborhood standards, you could sell for at (or below) typical market value and gain a profit.

5. Finally, the theory of *competition* is at the heart of valuation in real estate. The theory observes that when demand is stable, competition (other properties on the market) dilutes the potential

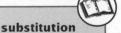

principle of regression
the theory of real estate valuation stating that higher-priced property values may be held back or even reduced due to their proximity to lower-priced properties.

highest and best use
a reference to property valuation, the observation that value is likely to be maximized when the property is used in the most suitable manner; and that values will be depressed when it is not utilized to its maximum potential.

substitution
the tendency for lower-priced properties to sell before high-priced properties with the same or similar features; and for lower sales prices to affect the market value of the remaining comparable properties.

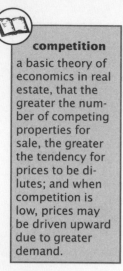

competition

a basic theory of economics in real estate, that the greater the number of competing properties for sale, the greater the tendency for prices to be dilutes; and when competition is low, prices may be driven upward due to greater demand.

profit for all available properties. Scarcity may drive prices up, and by the same argument, competition holds prices steady or may even reduce average sales levels.

Collectively, the various theories of valuation define how you need to evaluate market potential. It is not realistic to look at a particular property in isolation; you need to also consider the neighborhood and the prevailing conditions. The principles of conformity, progression, regression, highest and best use, substitution, and competition determine whether a particular investment is going to be profitable or not—just as the types of repairs a property needs, their cost, time to complete, and difference between asked price and property value define the viability of a particular property.

These principles can be thought of collectively as the basis for the fundamental analysis of real estate. In the stock market, the fundamentals refer to the financial aspects of a company, and analysis of those facts is used to decide whether or not to buy stock. In real estate, questions about current value and potential future value are similar. Not only is the current market price a consideration; the principles of valuation also have to enter into the picture in order for you to develop information to make an informed decision.

The Unattractive Property: A Quick Fix

Some properties can be quickly and easily repaired because the type of defects are strictly cosmetic. Considering the various supply and demand and market valuation realities presented in the last section, you have to expect to see a direct relationship between (1) the level of repairs required and (2) the margin of potential profit. This economic relationship is summarized in Figure 4.1.

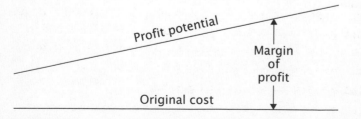

FIGURE 4.1   Relationship between profit potential and margin of profit.

What the figure demonstrates is the relationship between investment risk and potential reward. This relationship exists in every form of investing and is inescapable. In the stock market, higher-risk strategies may produce profits far above average, but they also come with much higher loss potential. In fixer-uppers, we apply this economic reality to better understand the "no-brainer," easy and fast cosmetic job, requiring only *lipstick repairs*, to one that is more complex.

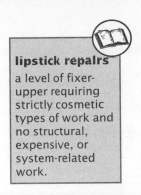

lipstick repairs
a level of fixer-upper requiring strictly cosmetic types of work and no structural, expensive, or system-related work.

So the more time and money you need to invest in a property, the greater the potential profit—to a point. You also need to be concerned about ending up with properties in which the required level of repairs is so great that you will not be able to make a profit at all. We need to revise the theoretical curve shown in Figure 4.1 to show that investing in an overly expensive property can cause net losses. The realistic curve is shown in Figure 4.2.

In comparing potential fixer-upper properties with the risk/reward factors in mind, remember these tips:

1. The easier, cheaper, and faster the work, the lower your likely profit margin is.

2. The maximum profit will be found in fixer-uppers that require extensive work, but only when that work can be completed without considerable extra costs.

3. When fixer-upper properties require expensive repairs, it will be increasingly difficult to make a profit because the repair levels exceed your net equity and market value after improvements. Remember the important equation:

$$S - [B + R] = P$$

This equation is translated as: Sales price at market value (S) minus the sum of your original cost basis (B) plus repairs (R), equals profit (P). So if this comes out to a negative, it will be a net loss. This equation is simple and obvious; however, it should be continually in your mind. The elements reducing your profit margin include:

a. Closing costs on both ends of the transaction

b. Interest expense, which will rise the longer you hold the property

c. Actual cost of repairs, including any expensive surprises

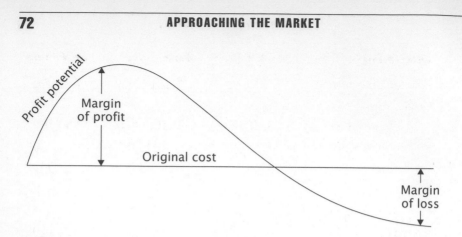

FIGURE 4.2 Profit and loss potential for a poor fixer-upper candidate.

If you make up a margin between your original basis and final market price with these three elements in mind, you can identify the most likely profit range for fixer-upper properties.

The "quick-fix" property is easy and inexpensive. But is it realistic to expect adequate profits to justify your efforts? Assuming you will put in time to make repairs, simply breaking even on a deal is not worth the time and risk. So you need to make enough profit to ensure you can justify the whole venture. A quick-fix property may be easy to repair, but it may only be practical if you plan to use the fix-and-hold strategy. Once repairs are completed, you rent out the property and earn positive cash flow; this is a fine strategy as long as it is intentional. Many fixer-upper investors end up stuck with properties they really do not want because they cannot get the price they need to cover their costs. Therefore, they have to wait out the market.

A quick-fix property is an excellent way to acquire positive cash flow properties as long as the numbers work out. In the situation where you simply buy a property to rent it out, you will be paying current market value. With a fixer-upper, however, the discounted value of the property is the key to positive cash flow. For example, consider the case where market rates for three-bedroom homes generally run at $125,000. Typically, rents for such properties runs about $600 to $650 per month. If you were to purchase a home at that price with a 30 percent down payment, you would need to finance $87,500. Monthly payments (based on a 30-year amortization at 7.25 percent) would be about $597. Now review a fixer-upper in the same neighborhood that is available for $100,000. Financing 70% would require monthly payments under the same terms of about $478. Assuming your needed repairs will run about $10,000:

Description	Market Rate	Fixer-Upper	Difference
Price of the property	$125,000	$100,000	$25,000
Cash outlay:			
Down payment	$37,500	$30,000	$7,500
Repair estimate	10,000	10,000	0
Total outlay	$47,500	$40,000	$7,500
Basic monthly cash flow:			
Rent estimate	$625	$625	
Mortgage	597	478	119
Net positive flow	$28	$147	

In this very preliminary sketch of the differences made in such a fixer-upper, the cosmetic repair strategy for acquiring rental property can improve your cash flow. In the previous example, you have $7,500 more cash in your pocket by buying discounted property. In exchange, you improve your monthly cash flow by $119, probably enough to pay for property taxes, insurance, utilities, and minor repairs and maintenance. The market-rate basic monthly cash flow (a comparison between rental income and mortgage payment) is marginal. It provides very little margin to pay for expenses above and beyond the mortgage. Even with tax benefits, the market-rate scenario would be difficult to maintain on a positive level. In comparison, the better monthly cash flow for the discounted fixer-upper property makes the idea viable. Also, when you consider the difference in down payment, you realize that your savings of $7,500 pays for three-quarters of your estimated repairs on the property. So your cash at risk level is more attractive in the quick-fix property—*assuming* that you employ this strategy specifically to acquire the property as a rental. If you want to flip the property as quickly as possible, you may need to consider buying fixer-upper properties whose repair level—and profit potential—are greater.

Creating a Budget

The methods you employ in evaluating potential fixer-upper properties have to include a budget of time and money. The time budget is important because interest expense can overrun your profit if your holding period is too long. The money budget defines whether or not the margin between basis and final sale can justify the risk. To prepare your time budget, you have to gain an idea of how long repairs are going to take. Some suggestions for controlling your time budget include:

Valuable Resource

Many free and low-cost catalogs and books about all types of home repairs are available from The Home Depot. This home improvement chain store is a good source for materials and tools as well. Check their website at http://www.homedepot.com/.

---

1. *Add a safety margin to your contractor's time estimates.* If you work with a contractor, get a clear estimate of time and then add a safety margin. You may even want to double the estimate, considering your contractor may have scheduling conflicts, materials could be delivered late, and inevitably work tends to take longer than the original estimate. This is why doubling the contractor's estimate is a smart idea.

2. *Be aware of possible weather restrictions.* Some repairs are going to be sensitive to weather. If it is exceptionally cold, painting, sheetrock work, and outside repairs or landscaping can be delayed. So timing your decision has to be coordinated with weather during the period in which you plan to hold the properties.

3. *Research specific repair times for work that you will do yourself.* How long does it take to tile a room, repair a roof, or remove brush and landscape a yard? If you plan to perform the work yourself, you may have no idea how long a job will take. One of the best sources for information is the contractor's desk at your local building supply store. Employees in home improvement stores generally tend to have a good idea of timing aspects to different types of repairs. These stores also may provide you with free brochures or low-cost how-to publications.

4. *Factor in your own time restrictions.* If you have a full-time job, when will you be completing repairs? If your time is limited to evenings and weekends, that will extend your time budget considerably and affect your overall profitability. The longer work takes, the more interest you will pay.

The time budget is not as tangible as a cost budget. You need to assess the cost of completing specific repairs. There are many sources for estimating costs. Here are some suggestions:

1. *Check your home improvement store.* The local home improvement store is often a valuable source for information. Where the big chains such as The Home Depot tend to have a lot of good literature, the smaller stores are likely to provide more expertise at the contractor's desk. Use both. The incentive to help you is in making sales, so you may find a lot of free assistance at local outlets.

2. *Search online for free calculators and estimators.* The Internet is loaded with unlimited numbers of free calculators and estimating systems. These are most useful for the repairs you are going to have trouble estimating. One of the most difficult is painting. If you simply go to your hardware store to buy paint, you will estimate the amount you need based on the house's size. But what about trim paint? Condition? Number of stories? All of these will affect your overall cost. So you may benefit from searching online for free calculation software; it could save you a lot of time and pin down an accurate and realistic budget.

Valuable Resource

A valuable online free calculator helps you estimate the cost of one of the most difficult improvements to budget: exterior painting. Check the Web site http:/www.contractors.com/ and click the Cost Estimator link. There you will find a calculator based on the property's measurement, number of structures, door, windows, and conditions. The calculator instantly gives you a dollar value for the cost of painting.

3. *Get estimates from local companies.* For work you are not sure about, get estimates from local contractors. This is useful not only because it gives you an idea of the costs involved; you may also conclude that it will be cheaper to subcontract the work. For example, if you are thinking of putting in an offer on a relatively large lot with a lot of dense brush that needs to be cleared, you have to consider the time and material costs of doing the work yourself. You will have to hire people and rent equipment. However, a local landscaping service may do the job for less time and money than it would cost you.

4. *Shop for bargains in materials.* What quality of materials do you need? For example, you can pay a lot for high-quality paint or stick with the low-cost bargain brands and restrict your selection to colors that are on sale this week. You can go to a specialty paint store or look for sales at Wal-Mart. The cost will be quite different between these possible outlets, and if you are buying 30 or 40 gallons of paint, it adds up. You need to define your intentions concerning quality of product as well. In a purely cosmetic property flip, you may only want to create a visual improvement without caring about long-term wear and tear. If you plan to convert a fixer-upper to a long-term hold, you may want to invest in higher-quality materials. You can shop for bargains and still find the quality and color that you want; but you need to decide in advance of preparing your budget what your policies should be about material quality.

5. *Remember, if you cannot pin down the cost, you could have a problem.* If you are thinking of putting in an offer on a property, but you cannot pin down the costs of completing repairs, it could be a danger sign. For example, if you talk to several contractors and each has a different idea of the costs involved, that is a sign that the real cost is probably going to be much higher than you are hoping. Get specifics. If you cannot, look at another property.

Checklists of Neighborhood and Properties

In determining which fixer-upper to invest in, you will need to undertake a thorough inspection and evaluation of your own. In addition to the professional, independent inspection you pay for, you will want to study the property's attributes to decide whether the needed work is a good match for your skills.

Be honest with yourself. Avoid the pitfall of becoming enamored with a particular property or type of property, to the point that you lose objectivity. Some rental income property investors mix up their objective investment analysis and their less rational but more emotional attraction to types of properties.

Example: A Lack of Objectivity

A husband and wife considered purchasing a house that was for sale by the owner. It was once a church and had been converted to two units. A second-story loft added the potential for two additional units. They asked their handyman to look at the property and to offer advice. They were not sure whether the level of needed repairs would justify the investment; the property had a lot of roofing, siding, paint, and internal problems and, to add additional units, it would require considerable investment of time and money. The contractor reported that the cost of correcting the property's problems would be over $25,000, far too high to justify buying. However, the wife liked the property and wanted to make an offer, in spite of the fact that the cost of improvements was far higher than the equity level of the property.

This is a difficult situation. The lost objectivity prevented one side of the couple from making an objective analysis and as a consequence, they could have sunk a lot of money into the property, never to recover their investment. Some properties are money pits and have to be avoided. If the level of disrepair is so severe that you could never recapture your basis (cost plus repairs), then it is not a sound investment.

Where do you start? Clearly, you need some type of list of features to look at. This list may serve the purpose of identifying potential problems and either rejecting a property or adding it to the list of possible fixer-uppers. The list may also serve as a means for developing important questions you will want to ask your contractor or inspector. You need to check both the neighborhood and the specific property. Table 4.2 provides a sample of the features that you should check when looking at a neighborhood. It raises a lot of questions and helps you to identify the *area* where you may seek fixer-upper properties.

Table 4.3 gets more specific. It is a checklist for inspecting a specific property. The various conditions of the property's systems can be checked off as needing attention. This provides you with a useful method for identifying potential problem areas. Some flaws will be obvious and others will not. The latter is where you need expert help from a contractor or inspector. Your goal is to ensure that your questions are answered thoroughly enough so that you will not have any surprises *after* you buy the property.

TABLE 4.2   Neighborhood Checklist for Fixer-Upper Properties

Area service
- ☐ Maintenance levels, public facilities
- ☐ Social service and volunteer outlets

Churches
- ☐ Availability
- ☐ Location

Crime
- ☐ Area safety and statistics
- ☐ Neighborhood watch programs

Employment
- ☐ Opportunities
- ☐ Trends
- ☐ Volume

Hazards
- ☐ Industrial sites
- ☐ Pollution
- ☐ Dangers

Home maintenance system
- ☐ Care taken by area homeowners
- ☐ Ongoing improvements

Parking
- ☐ Convenience
- ☐ Restrictions
- ☐ Street parking

Police
- ☐ Community involvement, reputation
- ☐ Proximity of stations
- ☐ Neighborhood patrols

Recreation
- ☐ Locations of parks
- ☐ Upkeep and condition
- ☐ Number of facilities

Schools
- ☐ Proximity, transporation provided
- ☐ Quality and reputation

Streetlighting
- ☐ Adequacy
- ☐ Future plans

Traffic
- ☐ Commute conditions
- ☐ Trends

Utilities
- ☐ Proximity
- ☐ Cost
- ☐ Restrictions

Child care
- ☐ Availability
- ☐ Reputation

Climate
- ☐ Average highs and lows
- ☐ Droughts or flooding

Cultural facilities
- ☐ Proximity
- ☐ Museums, libraries, theaters

Fire service
- ☐ Distance
- ☐ Statistics
- ☐ Quality

Health care
- ☐ Proximity
- ☐ Hospitals, doctors, emergency services
- ☐ Insurance plans accepted

Noise
- ☐ Airports, trains, highways
- ☐ Local traffic noise

Planning
- ☐ Buffers for other zoning
- ☐ Future plans
- ☐ Moratoriums

Privacy
- ☐ Arrangement of properties
- ☐ Landscaping
- ☐ Lot sizes and topography

Sales statistics
- ☐ Homes for sale
- ☐ Time on the market and trend direction
- ☐ Spread between asked and sold prices

Shopping
- ☐ Location and type
- ☐ Malls or districts

Terrain
- ☐ Steep slopes
- ☐ Wooded or other views

Transportation
- ☐ Public transit
- ☐ Cost and distances

Zoning
- ☐ Classifications
- ☐ Density
- ☐ Special assessments

TABLE 4.3 Home Inspection Checklist for Fixer-Upper Properties

Air conditiong system
- ☐ Age and condition
- ☐ Capacity
- ☐ Average cost to use
- ☐ Noise level

Basement
- ☐ Dampness or flooding
- ☐ Lighting
- ☐ Infestation

Chimney
- ☐ Loose brick
- ☐ Tilting
- ☐ Age and condition

Driveway
- ☐ Cracks
- ☐ Grading
- ☐ Staining

Floors
- ☐ Condition and materials
- ☐ Levelness or sagging

Heating system
- ☐ Age and condition
- ☐ Capacity
- ☐ Cost and efficiency
- ☐ Maintenance record

Landscaping
- ☐ Appearance
- ☐ Maintenance level and time
- ☐ Soil types

Plumbing
- ☐ Leaking or rusting
- ☐ Code compliance
- ☐ Water pressure

Screens
- ☐ Tears or holes
- ☐ Hinges
- ☐ Open and close condition

Utilities
- ☐ Public, association, or well
- ☐ Quality (water taste) and supply
- ☐ Septic maintenance and location

Appliances
- ☐ Age and condition
- ☐ Included or not
- ☐ Maintenance record

Brickwork
- ☐ Cracks
- ☐ Loss mortar

Doors
- ☐ Alignment
- ☐ Locks
- ☐ Age and condition

Electrical
- ☐ Capacity (220 volts)
- ☐ Code compliance
- ☐ Exposed wires

Foundation
- ☐ Cracks
- ☐ Evenness

Hot water system
- ☐ Age
- ☐ Type
- ☐ Capacity

Paint or siding (exterior)
- ☐ Age and condition
- ☐ Appearance and colors
- ☐ Loose pieces (siding)
- ☐ Warping (siding)

Porches and decks
- ☐ Conditions
- ☐ Material

Sidewalks
- ☐ Cracks or holes
- ☐ Levelness
- ☐ Age

Walls
- ☐ Cracks or holes
- ☐ Visible seams
- ☐ Water stains

Attic
- ☐ Dampness
- ☐ Insulation
- ☐ Infestation

Ceilings
- ☐ Cracks or holes
- ☐ Peeling or water stains

Drainage (gutters and downspouts)
- ☐ Broken sections
- ☐ Leaks
- ☐ Rotting (wood gutters)

Fences
- ☐ Age and condition
- ☐ Property line

Garage
- ☐ Size
- ☐ Construction
- ☐ Insulation

Insulation
- ☐ Amount and type
- ☐ Caulking
- ☐ Weather-stripping

Paint or wall coverings (interior)
- ☐ Age and condition
- ☐ Cracks or holes
- ☐ Peeling (wallpaper)

Roof
- ☐ Age and condition
- ☐ Curled or missing pieces
- ☐ Warranty

Stairs
- ☐ Loose handrails
- ☐ Loose treads

Windows
- ☐ Alignment and condition
- ☐ Cracks or breaks
- ☐ Rotting on frames
- ☐ Double-pane

Classifying Expenses: Cosmetic or Expensive

It is probably a wise idea to classify the types of improvements that you need to perform in one of three classifications:

1. *Purely cosmetic repairs.* These expenses can be done without expert help or a lot of material costs. And the time requirements will be short as well.

2. *Basic structural repairs.* These may require expertise and cost more money, but the cost and time requirements should be easily identified.

3. *Major structural or system repairs.* This classification is the most expensive and time consuming. Chances are that the majority in this group are going to be beyond your fixer-upper profit potential range.

Table 4.4 summarizes typical types of repairs in the three classifications. The cost-and-time analysis ultimately determine the level where you want to concentrate your investment—and the likelihood of creating a profit. For example, you might be willing to invest a lot of time and money to fully renovate a rundown property with good potential; but while the potential profits of such a high-level fixer-upper are high, so are the risks.

TABLE 4.4   Repairs by Classification

Purely Cosmetic Repairs	Basic Structural Repairs	Major Structural or System Repairs
Painting (exterior)	New siding (exterior)	
Painting (interior)	New wallpaper	
Vinyl tile flooring	Ceramic tile flooring	Hardwood floors
Linoleum flooring	New carpeting	
Window coverings	New baseboard	
Used appliances	New appliances	
Roof patching	Rain gutters	New Roof
Fix broken windows	Window upgrade	Window replacement
Landscaping (basic)		Landscaping (designed)
		Moving walls
		Upgrading plumbing
		Upgrade electrical
		Room additions
		Garage conversions
		Foundation repairs

The table is very general. Obviously, each property will have its own unique level of work needed to be done. For example, one house might need to have its siding replaced; another may have extensive water damage and rot beneath existing siding and eaves. The level of cost and time to fix these will be quite different.

Another attribute to be aware of in these three classifications is the level of visibility. The cheapest and easiest repairs—cosmetic—will make the greatest change in first impressions. By definition, these are visual fixes. The basic structural repair will improve appearances to a degree; but the relationship between cost/time and impression is diminished. The most expensive and time-consuming repairs—the major group—has the *least* first impression value. So from a strictly economic point of view, the cheapest and fastest repairs are going to be likely to return the greatest net profits. This assumes, of course, that you pick properties in the right neighborhoods, on the right block, and in the most advantageous market conditions.

The Buyer Psychology

In a sense, your efforts in fixer-upper properties take advantage of a tendency among the typical buyer: the desire to find and buy the "perfect" house. This is not to say that every buyer is lazy or unimaginative; but there is a very large market of potential buyers who share common attributes:

1. *They see what is there now, and not what used to be there.* You cannot realistically expect a potential buyer, seeing the property for the first time, to appreciate the transformation from its original condition. The buyer sees what is there. The fact that the house was unpainted and the yard overgrown will not interest the buyer, so do not expect to gain any advantage by emphasizing all of the work you have performed.

2. *They may be unwilling to recognize the value of needed cosmetic repairs.* When potential buyers look at properties, they have a buyer's eye and not an investor's eye. So the tendency is to see defects as negatives. A wise investor sees a cosmetic defect as an opportunity to negotiate a reduced price and to then perform repairs, gaining immediate appreciation as a result. A buyer may become concerned that an uncared for exterior could be a sign of hidden problems as well. While those concerns could be dispelled with a thorough inspection, the potential buyer might not be willing to even go to that extent.

3. *As buyers look at more and more properties, they may pay more attention (perhaps too much attention) to unimportant details.* Real estate agents notice a recurring pattern among potential buyers. As they narrow

their search, they become more and more concerned about unimportant details. They do not like the paint color, the angle of diagonal siding, the shape of the building, or the kinds of plants in the yard. With this in mind, you may want to keep your repairs and the property at a "minimalist" appearance level. Give the buyer less to find fault with, and help them to focus on value, potential, and appearance.

4. *Given the choice between a "perfect" house and one needing work, buyers are often willing to pay more for the property in better condition.* Buyers often are willing to pay more for a house that appears to need no work. They may shy away from an unkempt yard or a house needing a new paint job. Even when the cost of repairs is far less than the difference in price, buyers think in a particular manner, and that often makes no sense to someone else whose view is from the investment side. However, being aware of the tendency does help you prepare your property for the market with greater insight.

5. *Real estate agents want to close sales, so they appeal to buyers' emotions, not to their economic sensibility.* Real estate agents will encourage owners to clean up an ugly yard and even to paint a house, knowing that buyers are likely to be unable to look beyond the first impression. Agents do not want to have to convince their buyers; they would prefer to simply close the sale. The agent is likely to show a couple some specific features rather than emphasizing the "big picture" of value and markets. For example, an agent leads the wife to the kitchen while encouraging the husband to look at an area of the garage where tools could be stored or displayed. If the couple owns a boat, a large side yard is appealing; and if they have children, proximity of schools is important. All of those specific features are important, but they do not always point to the best values.

6. *For such a big purchase, many buyers decide impulsively or on minor details.* It is ironic that some people take more time and do market comparisons to buy a television set than they do for a house. Even though it is a big purchase (for most people, the biggest purchase in their lives), many buyers are impulsive. Remembering this, you may decide to concentrate on specific improvements. If the neighborhood is predominantly young families, for example, you might renovate the kitchen and repaint that dilapidated picket fence a bright, fresh white. The image of "home" resonates with many buyers, especially if the neighborhood is characteristic of where individuals and families see themselves living.

What this means to you as an investor is that opportunities may be quite good to turn a fixer-upper around for a short-term profit. However, you also need to review every neighborhood and every house individually. If your prospective property is directly across the street from a grade school, it will appeal to a family with young children; it will appeal less to an older couple with no children. If the property is located close to bus stops or train stations, commuters will consider that a plus; a self-employer buyer would be less interested in transportation, but far more interested in an extra room that could be converted into an office.

The character of the neighborhood and the mix of people living there will determine the type of buyer you are likely to attract. That is why the neighborhood checklist is essential to your fundamental analysis of the local fixer-upper market. With a particular target buyer in mind, you will find it practical to perform one type of repair or another. The market, after all, determines value *and* the profile of the likely buyer.

The next chapter explores yet another market strategy: combining fixer-upper properties with a long-term portfolio of positive cash flow rental income investments.

5

The Combo
Long-Term and Fixer-Upper Portfolios

A thorough evaluation of the two traditional methods of rental income property investing—buying and holding for rental income and buying fixer-uppers—clearly shows that both approaches have merit. Both have clear disadvantages too. Fixer-upper investing is not designed to benefit from long-term market trends, but dealing with tenants may involve cash flow risk. So which approach is going to be the most practical for you?

Most people do not fit conveniently into one classification or another. You may find that, given the advantages and disadvantages to each investment strategy, you may end up combining both in your investment portfolio. Some properties may be appropriate as long-term holds and others designed for fast in-and-out investment.

Investment Portfolio Planning for Real Estate

Every investor experiences superior market performance (success and profits) by performing sensible tests in advance. This is a preoccupation and often an obsession of investors in the stock market. Ironically, far less attention is paid to an analytical approach to selecting and owning rental income property.

discount
the difference between a fixer-upper's asked price and average market value of similar homes that do not need repairs or improvements.

The myth that you can make a profit on any property can lead to expensive mistakes. It is true that real estate values tend to rise across the board when market trends are upward; but the same is true in the stock market. Still, no one would suggest that any stock will be profitable. You need to pick real estate based on its investment attributes. These include the level of *discount* reflected in current price; level of repairs needed; potential profit from fast turnaround; cash flow; and long-term prospects for market value growth.

1. *Discount:* How much is the asked price of the property discounted from market value? This is an easy number to find; the typical property with the same attributes sells at the market average, and the fixer-upper property will be available for some level below the market price.

premium
a price higher than face value; in the case of real estate, if a fixer-upper's asked price is higher than the fair discounted market value, then that price is a premium above net market value.

2. *Repairs needed:* What is the cost of repairs? More to the point, is the repair expense lower than the spread between discount and market value? This is an essential question, but it often is not asked. If the repairs needed are higher than the discount, then it will not be worth your investment; taking repairs into the equation, the current price would reflect a *premium* over *net market value* (average market value *less* cost of repairs equals fair discounted market value).

3. *Profit potential from fast turnaround:* How long would you expect to keep a particular property, and what profit would you expect to earn upon sale? In evaluating several different properties, this question helps you to eliminate less profitable alternatives and concentrate on those offering the highest potential profit. The holding period is important because it affects the overall rate of return. For example, say you are comparing three different properties. Depending on (1) the amount of down payment, (2) your estimate of potential profit (the profit amount you think you will earn), and (3) the number of months you estimate you will own the property, the profit potential can vary considerably.

net market value
the true fair market value of property, represented by the difference between current market value less the cost of repairs.

Three examples are compared side by side in Table 5.1

TABLE 5.1   Profit and Yield Comparison between Three Properties

	Property 1	Property 2	Property 3
Down payment	$10,000	$15,000	$20,000
Potential profit	$ 4,000	$ 4,500	$ 5,000
Yield *(y)*	40%	30%	25%
Holding period (months) *(t)*	18	12	9
Annualized yield $[y \div t] \times 12$	27%	30%	33%

At first glance, you might be tempted to go with the property requiring the smallest down payment or the largest dollar profit. This can be deceptive. Because the down payment, estimated profit, and holding period vary between properties, you need to compute the *annualized yield*. This is calculated by dividing the potential profit by the down payment; this produces the yield. The yield is then annualized. In the three examples in Table 5.1, annualized yield is:

$$[\$4,000 \div \$10,000] \div 18 \times 12 = 27\%$$

$$[\$4,500 \div \$15,000] \div 12 \times 12 = 30\%$$

$$[\$5,000 \div \$20,000] \div 9 \times 12 = 33\%$$

Note how the outcome changes in these examples. The lowest down payment does not yield the best return; and the highest unadjusted yield actually results in the lowest annual yield, due to the length of the holding period.

4. *Cash flow.* The decision to decide to turn properties around quickly, or fix them up and then hold for long-term rental income, has to depend largely on cash flow. In the ideal situation, the discounted purchase price enables you to

annualized yield

the rate of return earned on an investment, calculated as if that investment were held for exactly one year. To calculate, divide the dollar amount of return by the dollar amount invested; divide the percentage by the number of months the investment was owned; and then multiply the result by 12 (months).

carry a small enough mortgage that cash flow will be very attractive. In that case, you create a healthy "hold" portfolio and you can justify keeping properties as rental income in your portfolio. However, if the level of rent would not justify the hold strategy, you may be better off trading on the discount and taking a gain, selling the improved property as soon as possible and moving on to another investment.

5. *Long-term growth prospects.* Just as stockholders hope to find stocks that will grow in value over time, you will want to find real estate with the same positive attributes. You may be unhappy with the current market price trends in real estate, in which case you will produce greater profits in turnover of fixer-upper properties. But if property values are outpacing other markets, it could make sense to adopt a hold strategy, at least for as long as the current trend continues. The evaluation itself will determine the more profitable strategy, based on current conditions in your regional real estate market.

A second aspect in portfolio planning is determining how to allocate your capital among dissimilar markets. Real estate naturally works as an allocation product offsetting the stock market. The trends in stocks tend to be opposite those in real estate, and vice versa. So many individual investors allocate capital between stocks and real estate, along with a minor third allocation of capital in liquid investments (savings accounts, money market funds, and short-term certificates of deposit, for example).

Within an allocation strategy, you will also want to diversify among many different products. Stock investors know they should not invest too much in one stock or even in stocks of one sector. The same is true in real estate, but methods of diversification may be more complex. You may not be able to invest in enough different properties to achieve true diversification; it may be necessary to find more subtle forms of diversifying your capital. For example, you can diversify between equity (owning property) and debt (lending money through second mortgages). You can also diversify by price, type of real estate (houses versus small apartment buildings or commercial buildings, or raw land, for example), or geographically—picking real estate in different neighborhoods or even towns or cities. You may also diversify by cash flow attributes: Raw land produces no cash flow and a residential triplex may produce superior cash flow, for example. When you go to different areas or towns, you may also find yourself diversified by market demand or by demand for rentals, which may be strong in one town and weak in another. Finally, combining fixer-upper ventures with long-term, positive cash flow rental income is also a form of diversification within the real estate market.

The analysis of these features—which define your portfolio strategy and ultimately your risk profile as well—is defined as the *fundamental analysis* of real estate. The study of the financial aspects and portfolio management features of properties you select, collectively determine how safe (or risky) your portfolio is, and how your capital is going to grow in response to various types of markets. When real estate values become more volatile, your market value will tend to be volatile as well; so diversification is a smart way to reduce the risk of loss, while recognizing that it also limits the potential rate of growth in market value.

The concept of "portfolio planning" does not belong exclusively to stocks. It is more properly defined as a long-term evaluation of *all* of your investments, including stocks, real estate, cash savings, retirement assets, and your own house. Portfolio planning should be approached with the desire to manage your capital for many years, and to identify the criteria for identifying and controlling risk profiles, the use of capital, and overall rates of return.

> **fundamental analysis**
> the evaluation of investments based on financial information. In the stock market, fundamentals are found primarily in the study of corporate financial statements; in real estate, fundamentals include an evaluation of market supply and demand, prices and discounts available, rental demand levels, and potential for long-term price appreciation.

Conversion: Fixer-Upper to Long-Term Hold

Your initial purpose in buying a property may be to fix it up and sell; but once repairs have been completed, you may decide to change your plans and convert to a long-term hold. As long as you are flexible and open-minded to this possibility, such a decision makes sense when:

1. *Cash flow is exceptional.* As long as you have positive cash flow, dependable tenants, and no pending repairs and maintenance, you may see holding as a low-risk idea. You may even have the desirable situation in which cash flow is positive but tax losses improve your tax situation (see Chapter 6).

2. *You want to keep properties indefinitely.* Some properties are best fixed and sold, and others are more desirable as long-term hold properties. If the neighborhood values are growing and if you believe that those values will be higher in the future, you may wish to wait out market growth. In the opposite situation—where you *have to* keep properties because a profit would not be possible in a slow market—you have a less desirable choice: Take a net loss or wait out the market in the hopes that values will improve in the future.

3. *Market conditions indicate that holding makes sense.* As long as you think there is a positive trend underway, holding can be the best alternative. This may be true because market values are growing, rental demand is strong, or both. The "market" for real estate has more than one aspect, so the whole picture should be reviewed to judge whether it is more sensible to keep properties or to sell as quickly as possible.

4. *You need the tax benefits, or want to defer reporting profits.* Your personal tax status will also affect your decision. You may have planned to fix and sell as quickly as possible; but your taxable income is higher than average this year. It could help keep your tax rate down to put off reporting a capital gain on property. Holding for extra time could also reduce your taxes if you want to get a long-term capital gain, which is taxed at a lower rate. So holding for 12 months could be a smart tax strategy. The same arguments work in reverse. For example, if you have a large capital loss in stocks this year, you can offset part of that loss by reporting a short-term gain on a fixer-upper sale. When it comes to tax planning, timing is crucial. Your goal is to reduce tax liabilities by coordinating and timing your reporting of gains and losses. This can directly affect when you want to sell your fixer-upper.

The conversion of a fixer-upper to a long-term hold is similar to decisions that you might make in the stock market. For example, you may buy stock with the idea of selling it in the near future, only to change your mind and decide instead to keep that stock in your portfolio. You need to remain flexible and to change your goals as new information develops. The same is true in real estate. Factors of tax benefits or consequences, cash flow, and your ever-changing perception of the market can all affect your timing. It is a mistake to assume one set of facts and to then remain unyielding in your policies. The markets and other conditions change.

For example, you might conclude at the end of performing repairs that positive cash flow will be stronger than you estimated and that converting the fixer-upper to a long-term hold is sensible. Replacing a temporary mortgage with a permanent, long-term mortgage may reduce your debt service and enable you to take cash out in some cases. That frees up capital to pursue other fixer-uppers. This works if and when you achieve positive cash flow and you want to keep the property. Some lenders are not willing to let investors remove cash upon refinance, and may not allow you to take out an equity line of credit on rental income properties. But with some research, you may be able to find sources for more liberal lending policies.

The need to get capital out and reinvest it often motivates fixer-upper investors to turn over properties as quickly as possible. The suggestion that you convert fixer-uppers to long-term hold status is premised on the availability of capital. In the ideal situation, your fixing-up expenses will improve property value enough so that you can remove most (or all) of your cash investment and use it elsewhere, while continuing to enjoy positive cash flow.

In theory, this concept—removing cash and acquiring ever-increasing numbers of property—is a road to real estate riches. Leverage, in which your capital is used repeatedly to increase your equity, is an exciting concept, but in practical application, this tactic does not always work out. You *may* be able to achieve the conversion on a zero-investment basis with some properties, but it will be the exception rather than the rule.

Conversion should be a conscious decision made when conditions warrant it. Going into the fixer-upper business on the assumption that you can leverage capital to the point that you own dozens of properties is far more difficult and not a realistic goal for most people. Cash investment levels can be leveraged—and getting the lending policies you need may depend on shopping around and locating more liberal lenders. Rarely is it easy to accumulate fast wealth in real estate by simply moving money from one property to another.

Fixing-Up Expenses in Conversions

There may be substantial differences in the types of repairs that you consider priorities once you decide to convert a fixer-upper to a permanent rental income property. This reality affects the way that you decide to prioritize repair work or the decisions you make about specific alternatives. The truth is, your willingness to invest money may depend on whether you are trying to appeal to buyers or to tenants. Consider the following examples:

1. *Floor coverings.* You might want to invest in attractive carpeting if you plan to sell. But if you are going to rent, you might prefer cheaper alternatives such as linoleum or vinyl tile; clean-up is easier and this flooring, while it may not be as appealing, is inexpensive.

2. *Window treatment.* As a near-future seller, you may decide to invest in high-quality, custom-made window curtains and blinds. If you plan to convert to rental income property, standard noncustom blinds will suffice. If you assume that tenants will cause greater wear and tear, it makes no sense to spend money on expensive custom-made items.

3. *Paint quality.* For the purpose of selling a house, a fairly cheap brand of paint will improve appearance while minimizing investment. If you plan to rent out the property, you may decide instead to spend more money to make the paint job more permanent, saving money in the future.

4. *Appliances.* You can spend a great deal of money on appliances if you buy new. But if you are planning to sell, those appliances are highly

visible. If you plan to include them with the property, you may want to buy nice-looking appliances to create the best impression. However, if you want to rent out the property, use working used appliances and spend hundreds less. Appearance is less important for tenants; saving money is a higher priority.

The timing of spending money on repairs and improvements should be set with the possibility in mind that you could turn the fixer-upper into a conversion. Put off spending money until you decide, for those items you will execute differently if you do decide to keep the property. While it generally makes more sense to give top priority to purely cosmetic improvements, some of these can be deferred. At some point, you will need to decide whether to put the property on the market, or keep it and rent it out. At the point you make that decision, your immediate priorities should be:

1. *If you plan to sell the property:*
   a. Get it listed immediately; start the ball rolling.
   b. Complete all repairs as quickly as possible that make a first impression (outside paint, landscaping, external repairs).
   c. Make final decisions about cost and quality for other repairs and improvements.
2. *If you plan to convert and keep the property:*
   a. Take action to get permanent financing if you are current under contract on a bridge loan.
   b. Reorganize the priority of repairs and improvements. Finish internal work so that you can place tenants as soon as possible.
   c. Once the majority of repairs are done, place an ad for a tenant. Begin interviewing immediately.

The decision to convert a property will change your attitude and priorities. In making this decision, be sure you consider the mortgage payment and overall cash flow; after-tax cash flow; market for rental demand; and long-term growth trends. All of these important factors should come into play when deciding to convert; and of course, the decision also changes not only the type of repairs and improvements you will complete, but the priority of those repairs as well. For example, if the property came with used appliances and you were planning to spend money on new replacements so the property would show better, you might decide to simply leave the used appliances in place. That decision alone could save $2,000 to $3,000 in the level of repairs. In making a side-by-side comparison between selling and holding, these types of cash outlay changes should be carefully considered; they affect the overall equation.

At what point do you make the decision? You could be undecided from the time you begin looking at properties, or the alternative might not occur to you until you begin completing work. Either way, be aware of the decision points. Before spending money on sale-oriented improvements, realize that it is expensive if you change your mind later.

Combining Both Types in Your Portfolio: Limitations and Guidelines

It may be practical to develop a portfolio of real estate that includes both fixer-upper work (short-term income) and rental income properties (long-term income). Even if you start out pursuing one strategy or the other, you may end up with both. The flexibility of switching back and forth gives you a market advantage; as various market indicators change, you can revert from short-term to long-term strategies.

Guidelines for the factors that will dictate which types of investments you emphasize include:

1. *Market supply and demand.* The basic equation will invariably determine whether it makes sense to hold property, or to sell. The interaction between supply and demand is changing constantly, and the market can move with little warning. So it is possible that you will buy a fixer-upper in a strong demand market, only to discover that a few months later, properties are not moving and the market has gone soft.

2. *Rental supply and demand.* Just as the market for real estate changes, so does the market for rental units. Factors affecting demand include competition (the opening of large apartment complexes in town, for example); economic change (a large employment base either leaving town or coming to town); and seasonal change (in areas with significant university population, for example, demand is going to be higher when school is in session under the semester system).

3. *Available financing terms and conditions.* You may be attracted to fixer-upper investments because you have found a good source for interim financing. However, if that source dries up or disappears, you may not find fixer-uppers as practical. As rates change for short-term (or long-term) mortgage money, the viability of fixer-uppers and the cash flow for rental income properties changes as well. The analysis has to consider interest costs, so you need to also consider this factor when trying to decide which property strategy to emphasize.

4. *Cash flow analysis or change.* Every real estate investor will succeed or fail on the basis of cash flow. If your after-tax cash flow is positive or

breakeven, you are in good shape. If cash flow is negative, you have to be able to afford to carry the investment, or you will have to sell. Unexpected events have everything to do with this question. For fixer-upper properties, higher than expected expenses, a soft real estate market, or delays in completion of work all affect the profitability of the venture. For long-term rental income investments, changes in rental demand, increased interest expenses, chronic vacancies, and unexpected repairs are typical of factors that affect cash flow. When these influences change, you will also need to review your basic real estate strategies. Cash flow may influence your decision to favor fixer-upper investing over long-term rental income, or vice versa.

Is one type of investing better than the other? It would not be fair to characterize fixer-upper or long-term hold strategies as "better" or "worse" because the decision has to be dictated by circumstances, individual preferences, available capital, and supply and demand factors. The decision is comparable to the decision investors make in the stock market. Would you prefer to buy stocks and hold them for long-term growth, or speculate on short-term profits and move money in and out of the market? That decision depends on your risk profile and attitude, as well as on current market conditions, Stock investors may switch back and forth or combine both strategies in their portfolio, depending on the mix of market conditions.

The same is true in real estate, although the decision is not always defined in terms of risk classification or profile, as it is in stocks. But even while the terminology is different, the comparison is valid. It may be reasonable to say that buying and holding real estate for the long term is conservative, and moving money in and out of fixer-upper properties is speculative. However, the attributes and conditions in each case can also change the risk levels considerably.

For example, if you invest in fixer-upper properties in a period of very strong market value growth, you may profit not only from cosmetic repairs but also from strong short-term market value growth. In this situation, fixer-uppers can be more profitable than long-term hold strategies.

As another example, if you hold properties based on assumptions about continuing high demand for rentals, your assumptions justify the decision, but only as long as the market conditions remain the same. The fundamentals of the conservative position can change. Softer demand leads to higher vacancies in some scenarios and the inevitable decline in cash flow makes the long-term hold less appealing. Continuing to hold may not make sense. But because the supply and demand for rentals and the market supply and demand may be quite different, opportunities can arise. You may be in a market of soft rental demand but very hot market demand. In this case, selling the long-term rental and reverting to a fixer-upper strategy could maximize profits while helping you avoid negative cash flow.

Living in Your Fixer-Upper

The problem of timing your hold period is aggravated when you are working against the clock. The longer you keep the property, the more you have to pay in interest. You may earn a profit, only to have the entire amount eaten up by interest on the mortgage. For some fixer-upper investors, the solution has been to live in the house while fixing it up.

The justification makes sense, at least on paper. You have to live somewhere and pay a mortgage, and moving from property to property while you perform repairs, takes a lot of pressure out of the equation. In fact, you have the luxury of time because there is no need to complete repairs quickly and put the property on the market. Repairs that could be completed in three months can be stretched out to six months or even a full year. You can put the property on the market when *you* are ready, and not on a predetermined deadline.

Another consideration involves tax planning. When you own your primary residence for at least two years, you can sell and pay no taxes on the first $500,000 of profits (for a married couple) or $250,000 (for single people). That is a comfortable margin and, if you can shelter your profits under the tax rules, it could be worthwhile to keep a property for two years.

The requirement that you use a property as your primary residence provides a good tax incentive, especially if your tax rate is high and if you need to avoid as much taxable income as possible. The primary residence requirement has to be given some attention, however, to ensure that your fixer-upper qualifies. The general rules to observe are:

1. *You must use the property as your primary residence at least two years out of the past five years.* This requirement means you have to identify the property as your primary residence at least 24 months to avoid tax on the profits. Is it always justified to keep the property two years? That depends on the level of profit, the potential tax liability, and your willingness to wait that long. If your priority is to turn over properties as rapidly as possible, it could make more sense to accept a lower profit rate and forgo the tax-free sale you would achieve by waiting two years.

2. *You can only have one primary residence at any given time.* The question arises, How do you identify a property as your *primary* residence? One important point to remember is that you can only have one primary residence at any one time. For example, if you own a vacation home

that you use two months out of the year, it is not your primary residence. It is entirely possible to have two primary residences during a five-year period; but you would have to physically move to a second property to set it up as your primary residence. Using a vacation home without moving there permanently does not qualify.

3. *There are a few clear methods to establish your primary residence.* You may have to prove that a property was your primary residence. You establish this based on where you receive mail, payments of utilities, and voter registration. These are good examples of methods you can use to document your primary residence. It is also important to identify a physical address on your federal tax return that is the same as the house you call your primary residence. If you are married, it makes sense that you and your spouse would have the same primary residence; so setting up one property for yourself and the other for your spouse will not get around this rule.

4. *You can claim the tax-free profit once every two years, without limitation.* The tax rules place no limitation on how many times you can sell a primary residence. You could move to a series of homes, wait two years, and sell without any tax consequences. However, you can only claim the tax-free sale once every two years. In cases where you have lived in two homes for at least two years out of the last five years, you could not sell both within a two-year period and claim the tax-free status.

5. *The period of occupancy does not have to be continuous.* The two-year rule is flexible. For example, you can establish a primary residence in one property for two years and then move to a second property for two years. In this case, both properties were your primary residence for at least two years during the past five years. You could sell either property and escape tax liability on the profits up to the limitations. But because you can only claim a primary residence sale as tax-free once every two years, you would want to time your decisions carefully to time the sale and to observe the five-year rule as well. Even beyond the example of moving from one residence to another, you could switch back and forth and still qualify—as long as you can establish that each property was used as your primary residence for the required time period.

Example: You purchased a home in January 2002 and lived there through February 2004. This was your primary residence. In February 2004, you purchased another home and moved your family into it, establishing a new primary residence. In March 2006, you decide you will sell one of the two properties. You sell the original home and escape taxes. You had used it as a primary residence from January 2002 through February 2004 (25 months). This occurred within the past five years. Two years later, in April 2006, you decide to sell the second property. You claim this as a primary residence sale and again complete a tax-free sale. You lived there at least two years out of the last five years; and more than two years have passed since the previous sale.

Personal Limitations

The concept of moving from one house to another may look good on paper, but in practice it could be impractical for any number of reasons. Whether you are considering a fast turnaround in ownership or living in a property for two years or more, you need to also think about how frequent moves affect your family. A second potential problem can arise from the stress of living in a property while you are completing repairs.

If you have children, the fixer-upper lifestyle could involve frequent moves between school districts and disruption of a child's life. Children have difficulty making friends when they move frequently, so the desirability of moving to new fixer-upper properties should be weighed against the importance of stability in the child's life. The same argument applies to spouses; you may believe that the plan is a good one, only to discover that your spouse is very unhappy with the prospect of being uprooted every few months.

To solve these potential problems, some people have tried to place tenants in homes they want to fix up and sell. This would also solve the problem of cash flow for a period of months, but you could be exchanging one set of problems for another, bigger set of problems. At the time you interview applicants for available properties, would-be tenants may tell you they have a problem with having work done on the property. However, many people are under pressure to find a place to live when they apply, and may tell you anything to close the deal.

Later, when a new tenant moves in, you could find that they resent having you around completing repairs, especially on the inside of the property. Their desire for privacy then overrides their original claim that they do not mind the disruptions. Subsequently, you find yourself in a high-stress situation in which tenants do all they can to prevent you from completing repairs. State rules require you to give notice before entering a tenant's premises, for example, and a tenant could demand that you give advance notice. They may even refuse entry, placing you in a difficult position. You may have offered the tenant lower than market-rate rent in exchange for cooperation. That makes no difference. You can both agree to special conditions, but if the tenant changes his or her mind, the law prevails.

When you eventually decide to sell the property, the tenant may further complicate matters. Real estate agents are also required to give advance notice, usually 24 hours. This is difficult when they have an out-of-town prospect wanting to see houses today. If your tenant, knowing that you are trying to sell, is confrontational with real estate agents and their clients, that makes it much more difficult to get a sale. If the tenant has not taken good care of the property, it will not show well, even after your fixer-upper repairs and improvements have been done. Some investors have come to the realization that it is better to give tenants notice and show the house empty, especially when these problems arise. The potential problems are made worse by real estate agents who do not respect the advance notice requirements. Many agents will show up unannounced with clients and ask your tenants to show the house. Agents may be aggressive and insistent and, of course, the tenant will be resentful toward you, the landlord, because of the imposition by the agent. So there are many potential problems involving tenants, not only when you want to complete repairs but also when you want to put the house on the market.

It may be an unfortunate truth that combining tenants with fixer-upper investments is not a practical idea. The cheerful, cooperative tenant does exist. However, you cannot count on always finding one, and when you want to put a rental income property on the market, you may have to give notice so the house can be shown empty. You avoid many potential problems in this way.

As you can see, when you go into the fixer-upper market or when you convert the property to a rental, you have many decisions to make. Making such decisions is complicated when you live in the property or rent it out during the short period of ownership. This requires tact and careful screening, and even after that you might still find yourself in a difficult position.

The next chapter introduces practical planning strategies that you need to employ when you invest in rental income properties. Your comprehension of market factors is a starting point; going forward with specific planning is the key to making your investment work profitably.

Part
2

Rental Income Investment Planning Strategies

6

Cash Flow First Aid

Stop the Bleeding, Do CPR (Cash-Positive Reasoning)

Perhaps the most expensive error any investor can make—in any market—is to commit capital without fully understanding the risks. In real estate, cash flow is more important than profits in the short term and intermediate term. Even if your real estate is eventually profitable, you need to get from here to there financially. This is where a study of cash flow is essential.

If you have invested in the stock market, you already know about risk. You know that it is easy to visualize the potential for profits without being aware of the possibility of losses. So many stock market investors gain experience the expensive way: by losing money. It is true that profits can be earned in the stock market, but stock investors have to be keenly aware that market conditions change rapidly and just as sudden profits can be realized, sudden losses can and do occur as well. In real estate, the situation is different in many ways. Real estate prices tend to move more slowly than stocks. The market is not liquid because you do not buy properties in an auction marketplace. A *ready market* of buyers and sellers does not exist like it does for stocks.

ready market
a market in which a high level of activity and interest are found, where buyers and sellers and quickly and easily execute trades, where margins may be thin; and in which changes in price levels may be rapid.

The attributes of stock market investing are based on thin margins of change. In comparison, you need a substantial margin between purchase and sale prices because the costs of moving in and out of real estate positions are high. You have to consider the commission, closing costs, and financing expenses as part of the overall equation. This means that to achieve a profitable position, you have to enter the market in one of two ways. First, you would plan to buy and hold real estate for a long period of time. Second, you would quickly fix up depressed properties to achieve a rapid margin of profit. In either case, the key to making the equation work is cash flow. The ultimate profit is important, but the immediate *requirement* that you achieve neutral or positive cash flow is more urgent.

How CPR Works

The phrase cash-positive reasoning (CPR) describes the process of analyzing real estate before entering an equity position. This is critical if you have any chance to avoiding a disastrous situation, one in which you are pouring money into the project without any immediate prospects of ever getting it back. So if your mortgage payment is $400 per month higher than your rent, you are experiencing negative cash flow. Not only is this a drain on your personal budget; it raises a disturbing question: *Is the property value increasing at a faster rate than your negative cash flow?*

You probably will not know the answer to this question and will have to estimate the answer. Because the whole idea of negative cash flow is unsavory, especially on a permanent basis, you will want to analyze your cash flow risk in advance, develop contingency plans, and ensure that any negative cash flow situations do not become permanent.

A study of cash flow should arise at several phases. These include:

1. *When you are comparing financing to rental income.* The first cash flow question should be: What are the monthly payments going to be versus the amount of rental income? This is a basic question because if the numbers do not work, the whole venture is questionable from the beginning. Remember, markets vary. In some markets, the cost of housing is so high that rental income investing simply does not make sense. This is especially true when there is a disparity between mortgage debt service and potential rents. For example, in San Francisco, modest houses may cost $600,000. If you were able to put $100,000 down and take on a $500,000 mortgage, your payments (assuming 30-year amortization at 6 percent) would be $2,997.75. At the level of value, property taxes and insurance will also be quite high. If we assume that your

basic monthly payments average $3,500 per month, can you expect to get that much in rent? Even if you can, a single-month vacancy could be a big problem, and a two-month vacancy or an unexpected repair could make the house unaffordable.

In other markets, housing prices may be relatively low but rental demand much higher. This is a far more desirable market for rental income property investing. For this reason the first cash flow evaluation has to be based on housing and rental market comparisons.

2. *When you consider the possibility of vacancies or nonpayment of rent and market demand levels.* The initial evaluation of debt service and likely rental income levels should be followed by a related study. In this second step, ask yourself what would happen in the event of an extended vacancy. In a high-level demand market for rentals, you may expect near-zero vacancy rates if your rental levels conform to market rates. If your property is vacant for two or three months, you will have to continue paying the mortgage without any offsetting rental income. While this fact is obvious, many would-be rental income property investors do not go through the cash flow analysis, and never ask this question.

A closely related risk is that you will have a tenant, but rent payments will not be made. How easy will it be to evict a deadbeat tenant? How long will it take? Will you need a lawyer? The time and expense of eviction can affect cash flow significantly. You will want to evaluate the landlord–tenant laws in your state to find out what the rules are and how much risk you face in having tenants occupying your property.

3. *When you budget for fixer-upper repairs.* For most people, arriving at a dependable budget for repairs and improvements is a daunting task. You may find yourself uncomfortable with the idea of estimating the

Valuable Resource

To find information about federal laws governing the landlord-tenant relationship, or to find the rules for your state, check http://www.law.cornell.edu/topics/landlord_tenant.html. To find specific rules in your state, type your state name in the search bar. You can also click the State Statutes link and select the desired state to review applicable rules and laws.

actual cost of work, and a little experience demonstrates that even a thorough evaluation often comes up short. How do you accurately and reliably estimate the cost of repairs?

It is essential to come down to a reliable number because you need to ensure that the properties you select can be turned over profitably. Missing the cost number often means losing money or having to hold properties longer than you would like. You could end up being an unwilling landlord because you cannot get your investment back out. With this in mind, you need to set specific limitations on how much you will spend. Jobs such as painting, landscaping, and flooring are usually not difficult to estimate, and many fixer-upper projects do not require more than these basic cosmetic jobs. Problems are likely to arise in invisible repairs such as unknown plumbing, electrical, and air conditioning problems, foundation heaving, and the like. Once you are serious about a house and its potential, take sensible steps to prepare your estimate:

- Ask the seller to pay for a home inspection.
- If the inspector's report includes hidden flaws, ask the seller to pay for them.
- Limit your repair work to tasks likely to return profits (cosmetics).
- Set a specific limit based on reasonable estimates.

You can determine the cost of fixing landscaping by asking for estimates from local landscape companies. If the job is simply a matter of clearing brush and bringing in fresh ground covering, you can do the legwork yourself and develop a fair idea of the cost. Floor coverings can be estimated based on evaluation of the cost per square foot of tile, linoleum, carpeting, and other coverings. Avoid expensive coverings such as hardwood floors; it is unlikely that you will increase the value adequately to cover this kind of cost. Paint estimates are fairly reliable based on a calculation of square footage and typical costs of paint by the gallon. In addition, use online calculators such as the one found at Contractors.com and consult with your local home improvement store (see Chapter 4). For big jobs, buy paint on sale and remember to include the cost of preparation as well as trim paint.

4. *When you set a target sales price and compare that to market conditions.* To justify the venture of buying the fixer-upper, you must have an idea of your target sales price. The original net cost—plus repair and improvement cost and the total interest you pay during the holding period—adds up to your investment basis. You need to sell the property at some level higher than that basis to justify the investment. Also be

aware of how much time you will have to spend performing work yourself. Is the profit worth the effort? If the margin is so thin that you end up working for one or two dollars per hour, perhaps you would do better getting a better-paying part-time job. In other words, the level of profits has to make sense in terms of the dollar amount *and* the time and effort you are required to spend. If the numbers do not work, look for different properties or wait for more favorable market conditions.

Studying the Essential Cash Flow Problem

Mastering cash flow and anticipating—thereby avoiding—cash flow problems are part of *risk management* in real estate investment. Stock market investors are preoccupied with price movement of stocks, and this is appropriate. Stocks can change value rapidly; so both profit and loss can occur in a matter of days or even hours. In the stock market, market risk is the primary high-priority concern. For this reason, investors diversify and invest in stocks with low volatility. But in real estate, market risk is a secondary concern. Once you have identified real estate with strong potential to hold its value and to grow in value over time, a more immediate concern becomes cash flow. The question of how to evaluate and control cash flow is the most important aspect of owning rental income property.

risk management the process investors use to evaluate, control, and reduce various forms of investment risk; the methods by which exposure to loss is controlled while potential for profits are kept in place.

The evaluation of risk is never the same; it has to be altered to fit the circumstances. Between different markets (such as stocks or real estate) we know that the attributes or price units, market liquidity, volatility, and availability of the market itself all make these markets vastly dissimilar. Within the real estate market itself, risk evaluation is based on the cash flow margin; market and rental demand; estimating holding period; cost of repairs and improvements; and in the case of rentals, the strength or weakness of the rental market.

For example, if you are considering buying one of two or three potential fixer-upper properties, the types of questions that would allow you to make valid judgments concerning profitability and cash flow would have to include:

- Cost of the property and recent price trends in the area
- Financing available on today's market
- Down payment required
- Closing costs upon purchase and sale of the property
- Type of repairs needed

- Expertise needed for repairs (requirement to hire others or complete work yourself)
- Estimated cost of repairs
- Estimated holding period
- Likely net profit
- Rental market rates (if you plan to keep the property for rental income)

Table 6.1 is helpful as a checklist for this comparison.

TABLE 6.1   Property Evaluation Worksheet

Description	Property 1	Property 2	Property 3
Property cost			
Recent price trends (strong, moderate, or weak)			
Financing terms:			
Number of points			
Interest rate			
Bridge loans			
Amortization term			
Down payment required			
Closing costs:			
Purchase			
Sale (estimated)			
Type of repairs needed:			
Yard			
Outside paint			
Inside paint			
Floor coverings			
Window coverings			
Appliances			
Kitchen			
Bath			
_____			
_____			
_____			
Expertise needed for repairs (high, medium, or low)			
Estimated cost of repairs			
Estimated holding period			
Likely net profit			
Rental market rates			

These critical evaluation points make the most sense when compared between properties. The worksheet on Table 6.1 is helpful as a checklist for this comparison.

A comparison between properties of the "risk attributes" defines cash flow risk. If the costs are high and potential profit margins are low, it leaves little room for the unexpected. Anyone working on a fixer-upper knows that unpleasant surprises occur often. Those who work with tenants know that vacancies may only be the beginning point in cash flow risk. Difficult tenants who do not pay rent or who destroy property can be just as expensive as vacancy-generated negative cash flow. All of the potential causes of cash flow problems need to be identified; in choosing from among several properties, you will improve your selection by going through the checklist and picking the properties that hold the greatest potential.

Such properties often are the most run-down in appearance. A low-cost series of cosmetic repairs not only cost little and do not take a lot of time; they also can vastly improve property value rapidly. In comparison, more expensive, time-consuming repairs may not return the same profit on capital invested. Time is an important element in the equation. If you are making payments on a mortgage, the clock is ticking on a daily basis. The longer you delay selling the property, or the longer it takes to complete repairs, the lower your profit.

Guidelines and Suggestions: Managing the Profitable Situation

To ensure that you develop the expertise to pick fixer-upper properties or rental income properties to maximize profits, you need to pay close attention to *immediate* cash flow. The strength of the housing, financing, and rental markets is crucial, of course; but even in the best of conditions, if cash flow does not work out, you could have big problems. To create and manage your investments to create consistently positive results:

1. *Take all the time you need to make your comparisons.* The decision to invest in rental income property is going to involve commitment of funds and a large amount of debt. This decision should not be entered lightly. If you invest in 100 shares of a $20 stock, you risk $2,000, which is not a small amount; but that is the extent of your risk. If you make a $20,000 down payment on a $100,000 property, that is 10 times more cash *and* a commitment of $80,000 in debt. Therefore, your credit rating and financial health depend on making smart decisions. Even so, some people give in to pressure from aggressive real estate agents or perceive that they have to make fast decisions or miss

opportunities. Be as methodical as you need; check the attributes of each property and do not proceed until you are certain that you are making a smart decision.

2. *Consider* all *of the elements affecting cash flow.* Potential growth in market value is the most common reason that people go ahead and invest in rental income property. They want to get a piece of the action when markets are hot and property values are rising. But even if you are right about the health of the real estate market, you need to look at the bigger picture. What are local vacancy rates? Can you afford to make mortgage payments if the property is not rented out for a month, or even for longer? Are you confident that your estimate of repair costs is reasonable and complete? Have you seen a home inspection report, and are you certain there are no hidden flaws? Are market rents adequate to cover your mortgage payment, property taxes, insurance, utilities, and other expenses?

3. *Seek acceptable positive cash flow margins.* It may not be enough to have "just enough" cash flow to break even. In that scenario, an unexpected vacancy or repair bill creates an automatic negative cash flow outcome. In comparing between properties, seek those in which the difference between market rents and likely monthly payments is comfortable. If you locate fixer-upper properties available well below market prices, it is one way to create positive cash flow (market rates should be adequate to cover the mortgage). It may also be necessary to make a larger down payment to ensure a comfortable cash flow margin.

4. *Determine in advance whether you want a fast sale or a long-term hold. This will affect the types of properties you buy, the repairs you identify, and the financing you seek.* It is a good idea to always set investment goals for yourself, including your purpose in buying rental income property. There are different profiles of investors. Are you looking for the fastest possible turnaround? Are you planning to live in the property? Do you intend to fix up the property and then hold it as a rental? If so, for how long do you plan to hold? All of these questions affect the kind of properties you look at and the level of price you will be willing to pay. You need to establish your investing policies and goals before looking for real estate. It is a mistake to begin by seeing what is on the market.

5. *Pick your target purchase price, sale price and date.* Once you know what your plans are for rental income property, you will be able to further define what you're looking for. Pick a sales price and target sales date. If you seek a fast turnaround, you may even want to put the property on the market fairly soon after you close your purchase, to attract potential buyers. This works when the purely cosmetic repairs can be done very

quickly. How do you know how to pick a purchase and sale price? If you want to achieve a fast turnaround, it is straightforward. You need to identify a *margin of profit* between the two sides. On one side is your net purchase price, interest and other expenses during the estimated holding period, and the cost of improvements. On the other side is the net sales price. This margin of profit has to be high enough to justify the risk. If it is minimal, what happens if unexpected repairs show up, or if the work takes longer than you thought? Even if you cannot find a buyer quickly enough, ongoing interest expenses can quickly absorb a minimal profit, so you need to put a lot of thought into the estimated margin. Use the worksheet in Table 6.2 to calculate your estimated margin of profit.

> **margin of profit**
> the difference between your investment and sale prices. Investment basis consists of original price plus closing costs; repair and improvement expenses; and interest expense on the mortgage. Closing price is the net amount received after closing costs. Margin of profit is expressed as a percentage of the investment basis.

There are two methods for calculating the margin of profit: dollar amount and percentage. Both are important. Furthermore, if the holding period on the properties you are comparing is not identical, you also want to annualize the yield to make it comparable. For example, say that you are considering three different properties. Your estimated margin of profit is 16, 22, and 11 percent. Your holding period is estimated on these three as 6, 12, and 3 months. To annualize, divide the estimated yield by the number of months in the holding period and then multiply the result by 12 (months):

$$\text{Property A: } [16 \div 6] \times 12 = 32\%$$

$$\text{Property B: } [22 \div 12] \times 12 = 21\%$$

$$\text{Property C: } [11 \div 3] \times 12 = 44\%$$

Because the estimated holding period is dissimilar among these three properties, the comparison is unreliable unless you annualize the yield. In this example, Property B (with the initial estimated yield at the highest level, 22 percent) ends up the least profitable; and Property C, which had the lowest apparent yield, would produce the highest annualized yield.

TABLE 6.2   Margin-of-Profit Worksheet

Description	Property 1	Property 2	Property 3
Market price:			
Original price	$	$	$
Closing costs			
Interest expense, ___ months			
Cost of repairs:			
Yard			
Outside paint			
Inside paint			
Floor coverings			
Window coverings			
Appliances			
Kitchen			
Bath			
_____			
_____			
_____			
Utilities			
Total Basis	$	$	$
Sale price target			
Closing costs			
Net Sale	$	$	$
Margin of Profit	$	$	$
% Profit	%	%	%

6. *If you discover that additional work is needed, think before you proceed.* Once you own a fixer-upper, there is always the chance that (1) additional work is needed that you did not include in your original estimate; (2) the work takes longer than you thought; or (3) the work costs more than you originally believed. In any of these circumstances, revise your original estimate and reevaluate the margin of profit. Finding out

that your numbers do not work out as you thought is not a sign of poor judgment; it is part of the risk profile for rental income investing. You will find that with experience and with thorough analysis up front, the extent of extra work and higher costs will be minimal. However, the decision to proceed with work has to be based on a realistic assessment of the margin of profit. You do not want to spend so much money that it becomes impossible to earn a profit. In that case, you either have to accept a loss or hold the property longer than you want to. Neither of these scenarios is attractive, so consider a third alternative: putting the property back on the market without performing all of the repairs. If the surprise discovery of needed repairs was not part of your original equation, you can still make your margin of profit without spending more time or money. If the repair did not show up in your home inspection or your own evaluation, it may not fit the profile of the type of repair you need to perform.

Unplanned circumstances can also enter the picture. For example, the fence falls down during a windstorm and your insurance company does not cover it because the fence posts were weakened over time. In this situation, you have a choice: Either repair the fence and spend money you had not planned to spend, or remove the fence altogether. Having no fence makes the land appear larger because the view is expanded, so its removal can be a smart marketing decision as well as being a cheaper alternative.

7. *If the numbers are not working out, sell the property and accept a loss.* Not every investment is profitable. Whether you put your money in stocks, mutual funds, real estate, or somewhere else, you are going to suffer some losses. It does not make sense to keep losing investments and, in the case of real estate, it can get quite expensive—especially if your cash outlay is not keeping pace with increased market value. With experience, you can reduce the level of losing ventures. But one bit of wisdom worth remembering is: If the numbers are simply not working out, cut your losses as quickly as possible. Put the property on the market, and stop the negative cash flow as soon as possible. There is no value in holding onto property that is losing money every month. You benefit from the "experience cost" of the loss—and all investors go through such experiences. One myth surrounding real estate is that *all* investments in rental income property are profitable if you hold them long enough. A more sensible rationale is: You need to compare cash flow to potential market growth to decide whether it makes sense to keep properties that are not performing well.

Cash Flow and Fixer-Upper Time Restrictions

Even if you have a specific and realistic grasp on the costs involved with repairs, will your fixer-upper be profitable if repairs take too long, or if you cannot find a buyer as quickly as you would like?

The holding period is as important as the cost of repairs. Your ongoing interest expenses can be substantial and, unless you are renting out the property while you complete repairs, it is a complete drain on cash. For example, a $100,000 mortgage at 6 percent with a 30-year amortization will cost you about $500 per month. So if you plan to sell the property in four months from closing date, that is a $2,000 cost; but if you end up keeping the property eight months, interest costs double to about $4,000.

How do you estimate the holding period? The estimate has to include two major segments: (1) the time required for completion of repairs and (2) the time required to find a buyer and close the sale. The time requirement for completion of repairs is difficult if you have not had experience with similar repairs in the past. How long does it take to paint the exterior of a house, replace a floor, or replace kitchen cabinets? Even clearing brush from a yard may be difficult to pin down in terms of how much time it will take.

Ask questions. You can check with experts in the field such as landscapers, contractors, and knowledgeable people at your local hardware store. If the store has a contractor's desk, this is a good place to start. You do not have to be a contractor to ask questions. Find a time when the store is not especially busy and ask your questions. You can also consult with experts in specific departments. Most large hardware stores are arranged by section, and many have employees who can answer questions about specific projects. The large chains may not be as helpful because they hire employees who primarily know where things are in the store. They may know next to nothing about your project. At the same time, if you find the right person, you can get a lot of information. Some employees in large chain stores such as The Home Depot have a vast amount of knowledge, and they tend to be found specializing in one department (see Chapter 4). Local hardware stores tend to charge more for their products, but may also be far more helpful. Your primary question should be: "How long is it going to take me?"

Add some time to the estimate. If you are inexperienced, you may not be able to complete a task in the same amount of time the expert tells you. It might take an experienced person one hour to complete a task. They have done it many times and they know exactly how to prepare the surface. But you have to allow for a learning curve. For example, if you are replacing a broken window, what do you need to know? It could take you twice the time an experienced person needs. You have to know how to measure the area; remove loose grout and scrape the area; and ensure that the frame is secure and not loose. You

Valuable Resource

To get answers to common repair questions, check http://www. handymanusa.com/ and click the link for the desired topic of interest. For example, if you click the Doors and Windows link and then click Window Glazing, you find step-by-step instructions.

also need to know what to buy in addition to the glass. What holds it in place, and how is it applied? What kind of putty should you buy? What are glazing points, and how are they used? What tools do you need?

You can find the expert help you need, not only with estimating the time requirement, but also with how to do the job itself. In a short amount of time, you will gain the experience to know how long you will need to complete specific repairs. You learn a lot by doing the work. Remember these guidelines:

1. *Add time to any estimates you receive.* Most estimates assume experience and knowledge. They assume that nothing will go wrong. You should add extra time to ensure that you do not fall behind schedule.

2. *Overlap jobs to increase efficiency.* You do not have to complete only one job at a time. Get as many projects started as possible. For example, you can do landscaping work during the day and begin painting the inside rooms in the evening. If you hire others to help, there is no reason they have to be lined up one after the other; get as many projects going at the same time. As long as people are not going to be in each other's way, and as long as performing a task does not depend on someone else finishing their part first, you can have multiple tasks going on at the same time. So if you have seven tasks, and they take one week each, that does not mean you need seven weeks for completion. You might be able to get through the list in three weeks, perhaps less.

3. *Perform extensive research.* Become an expert on the repairs and improvements you want to perform. Set up files. The information you get today will be useful not only on this job, but also on future jobs. Talk to contractors and other experts. Get written estimates. Establish working relationships. Every fixer-upper investor should know at least one carpenter or handyman, electrician, plumber, roofer, pest control service, and home inspector—as a starting point. The more resources you have at your disposal, the better.

4. *Get second opinions.* Never accept the first estimate you get, without getting a second estimate. And if someone tells you that you can paint your entire house in less than one day, ask someone else. Get many estimates, both for cost of materials and labor, and for time requirements. Be sure you know what to expect by checking around and by learning whose estimates are reliable.

5. *Ask questions at your local hardware store.* The local handyman store is perhaps your best resource for information. Many employees in these stores have a vast store of knowledge (and of course, some just work there and are only good to tell you which aisle to look on). Providing information to customers is smart marketing. Management knows that if you get good information, you are also likely to buy tools and materials in their store. So shop where you get the best information and help.

6. *Search for how-to information online.* Do not overlook the Internet as a source for information. You will find a vast range of helpful information about cost of materials, how jobs are completed, and what tools are involved. From this range of data, you will also get a fair idea of how long the job is going to take.

The second factor making it difficult to estimate your holding period is finding a buyer and closing the sale. How long does that take? The answer depends on how much effort your agent puts in, and how many buyers are available. Some real estate agents just collect listings, put up a sign, and depend on other agents to check the Multiple Listing Service (MLS). Others aggressively look for buyers. Here are some ideas:

1. *Shop for agents.* Do not settle for a passive marketing approach. Look for an agent who is known for closing a lot of sales. Avoid agents who just list properties but do not actively work with potential buyers. Ask your banker for referrals; look in the paper for names that show up on a lot of listings and open houses; look for agents who have been named as top producers.

2. *Provide incentives to the agent to find a quick sale.* In some listing agreements, you may be able to include a compensation bonus or other incentive. For example, your agreement may specify that you will pay a 6 percent commission, but an additional 1 percent will be paid if a buyer is found within 30 days (and that buyer ultimately closes the deal). You may also specify a higher commission rate if a sale is

generated within the agent's brokerage firm. You can also place incentives in the commission structure. For example, the contract may specify that the commission is 6 percent of the first $100,000 and 3 percent on the balance. This varied commission rate structure opens up the possibilities for fast-sale incentives.

3. *List your property before you complete your repairs and improvements.* You do not have to wait until all of the work is complete to list the property. Plan the timing of your listing, remembering that it takes time for the real estate market to move. Having your listing on the MLS with a photograph is helpful; but it could take several weeks until prospective buyers begin to show interest. Once your outside cosmetic repairs have been completed, get your agent working on a listing agreement. Complete inside repairs while the listing is active.

4. *Think about the pricing of your property.* Every real estate agent knows that a property can be priced in various ways. There is the *fast sale price*, a discount from the *fair market value* of the property. This price is designed to attract a buyer as quickly as possible. This is based on the assumption that buyers will recognize a bargain. Some sellers have a *firm price* in mind, meaning they are in no hurry and will not negotiate. Agents may ask you to accept a discount because they have a *cash buyer* in the wings. It seems that every real estate agent knows a cash buyer, but in reality, cash buyers are rare. Once you set a price, do not be swayed by the promises made by real estate agents. Your price should be set according to reasonable market values, and by how quickly you hope to find a buyer.

5. *Anticipate questions; reduce closing time by getting your own inspections and appraisal.* The closing time requirement depends on many steps.

fast sale price
the price for real estate set to get a fast sale; a discount from fair market value established to close as quickly as possible.

fair market value
the realistic and competitive price for real estate on today's market, based on average sales for similar properties in recent weeks or months.

firm price
the price set by a seller who is not willing to accept a discount; a price based on fair market value, usually indicating that the seller is not in a hurry to find a buyer or to negotiate the sales price.

cash buyer

anyone who plans to pay cash for property, and who will not need to go through financing qualification. Real estate agents often persuade sellers to list with them because they claim to have a cash buyer, meaning the deal could close quickly. In practice, few cash buyers exist.

Sellers need to get financing approval and, if they cannot, the sale will not go through. Other contingencies that hold up a sale include the time required to complete inspections and an appraisal. You can cut down on the delay by getting your own inspections and appraisals and making reports available to serious sellers. This achieves two advantages. First, it eliminates the contingency that an inspector may find a hidden flaw. Second, it cuts down on the potential delay. In some areas, inspectors or appraisers are extremely busy. When interest rates are low, a high volume of refinancing places a burden on experts, especially appraisers. So if you can arrange these ahead of time, you cut back on the required escrow period. A buyer may want to get independent inspections and a bank may require its own appraisal. However, having these performed in advance does help to speed up the whole process.

Calculating Rental Property After-Tax Cash Flow

If you plan to invest in fixer-upper properties, your primary emphasis is going to be on time and cost. You need to coordinate timing as well as picking discounted properties. The task is different if you want to invest in rental income property that you plan to hold for the long term. In that case, your emphasis will be on ensuring that you will be able to create positive cash flow.

Because tax benefits are a significant part of the real estate cash flow equation (described in Chapter 7), you need to include tax benefits in your cash flow calculations. Table 2.2 in Chapter 2 provides an example of how after-tax cash flow is calculated. This calculation is complicated because:

1. *Tax benefits are significant.* The tax benefits in owning rental income properties are substantial. But the rules are complicated, as we show in the next chapter. In calculating annual or monthly after-tax cash flow, you need to be aware of your federal *and* state effective tax rate; limitations on the deductibility of real estate losses; and which payments are deductible versus those that are nondeductible.

2. *Depreciation is a noncash expense that you are allowed to deduct.* Calculating depreciation is important to every rental income property investor. It is a major expense but it is not a cash expense. When you buy

property, you are allowed to claim an annual deduction for depreciation on the building and other improvements (but not on land). This deduction reduces your tax liability even though you are not specifically paying money out each month. In effect, depreciation doubles up your deduction because you can also claim interest expenses, which represents the lion's share of your mortgage payment. This noncash deduction is the key to your real estate tax advantage. It is possible, due to depreciation, to create a situation in which you claim a net loss for tax purposes, but you have an overall positive cash flow.

3. *Debt service includes deductible interest and nondeductible principal.* Part of your mortgage payment is deductible. Part is not. You can deduct all of the interest you pay, which is most of your payment during the earlier years of the mortgage term. You need to be able to estimate the year-to-year breakdown, however, because the nondeductible principal segment of the mortgage payment increases each year, offset by reductions in interest.

4. *Property taxes and insurance payments usually do not occur every month.* Payments of property taxes and insurance are made in one of two ways. If you make these payments yourself, you probably pay twice per year; some insurance plans are paid with a single annual premium. If your mortgage payment includes taxes and insurance (known as PITI, or principal, interest, taxes and insurance) then part of your monthly payment goes to impounds, accounts set up by lenders to collect tax and insurance and then make periodic payments. As far as cash flow calculations are concerned, the total mortgage payment represents a cash outlay, but the deductible totals for taxes and insurance are based on actual liabilities. The withheld amounts may not be identical to the tax deduction amounts.

5. *Capital improvements are cash outlays that are not deductible in the year paid.* When you add rooms, replace appliances, cabinets, flooring, roofing, and perform other major repairs, you are not allowed to claim a deduction in the year the cash is paid out. These capital improvements are set up as fixed assets and depreciated over a period of years. So as part of your cash flow calculation, you have a cash outlay for capital improvements; but you can only deduct depreciation over several years, not all at once.

Cash flow calculations do not have to be complicated. However, you do need to understand the rules for (1) tax computations, (2) depreciation, (3) limits on annual deductions, (4) timing of property tax and insurance payments, and (5) calculations and breakdowns of mortgage payments. It is possible to project cash flow over two or three years, but the further out the estimate, the less reliable the projection. The purpose in performing cash flow calculations is to compare properties and to ensure that market rents are going to be adequate to cover known expenses as well as nondeductible payments. This includes capital expenditures and principal on your mortgage loan. You also need to be aware of the tax benefits you will gain by owning rental income property, because those benefits often make the difference between overall positive or negative cash flow.

In the next chapter, tax rules for real estate are summarized and explained. While you should be aware of all of the rules, remember that rental income investing involves special limitations and benefits. You should plan to consult with a tax expert to plan out your investment program with the tax rules in mind.

7

Taxing Matters
Inevitable but Advantageous

Most people find federal and state taxes overly complex, requiring professional help each year. When you become involved in rental income property, it becomes even more complex. Many rules apply only to real estate, such as a provision allowing you to deduct losses each year up to $25,000. Other types of investments allow you to deduct losses only to the extent that they offset other gains; or in the case of capital gains, limited to only $3,000 per year. So real estate investors get special benefits.

The rules are also restrictive in many ways. You must establish that you are actively involved in managing your properties as a condition of claiming tax losses. You need to master the rules of depreciation. And you also have to plan ahead, especially if you convert rental income property to your primary residence or vice versa.

Even when you use outside professional help—and this is strongly advised—it makes sense to be aware of the rules, benefits, and restrictions. Knowing how the tax rules work makes it easier for you to plan ahead. When you buy and sell rental income property, you may wish to consult with your tax adviser two or three times a year, and not just when you need your tax returns completed. In addition to completing the returns, you also need the *tax planning* assistance that a qualified

tax planning
a form of financial planning with taxes in mind: timing of purchases and sales, offsetting capital gains and losses, and identifying tax benefits. Planning is also essential to identify deductibility limits, make appropriate depreciation elections, and identify the after-tax cash flow and profits from rental income investments.

119

professional can provide. A caveat: This chapter is by no means a comprehensive explanation of real estate tax rules. It provides an overview of the rules you need to know, and how those rules may affect your rental income investment decisions.

Real Estate Tax Rules

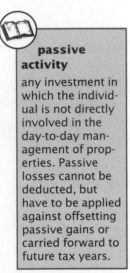

passive activity

any investment in which the individual is not directly involved in the day-to-day management of properties. Passive losses cannot be deducted, but have to be applied against offsetting passive gains or carried forward to future tax years.

active participation

status of investors in rental income properties when they make decisions concerning tenant selection, rent levels, repairs, and buying or selling; active participation is a requisite for deducting annual net losses from rental income activity.

Three specific tax rules are unique to rental income investing: passive loss limitations, annual loss deduction limitations, the requirement for active involvement, and limitations based on your adjusted gross income.

A *passive activity* is defined as a form of investing in which the individual is not directly involved in the day-to-may decisions. Typical passive loss activity includes real estate limited partnerships, in which general partners manage properties and limited partners only contribute money. Because limited partners are not involved in management and decisions, any passive losses cannot be deducted; they have to be applied against passive gains or carried forward and used in later tax years.

Rental income investments *may* be classified as passive losses. If you are not directly involved in making decisions (such as approving tenants, collecting rents, and completing repairs) you may not be allowed to deduct net losses under the passive activity rule. You need to be able to show that you are directly involved to claim losses.

You need to meet two tests to claim net losses on rental income investments. The first test is called *active participation*. This means that you need to be involved in interviewing and picking tenants, dealing with any questions or problems, completing maintenance and repair work or supervising someone you hire, and deciding which properties to buy or sell. The second test is called *material participation*. You have to own at least 10 percent of the property to be treated as a "material participant," meaning one who is allowed to claim net losses. If you own only 5 percent of a property co-owned with other people, you cannot claim any net losses. You have to meet with active and material participation requirements to claim net losses on your tax return.

With these rules in mind, rental, income investments may be treated strictly as passive activities, or as
active. If they are passive (meaning you do not meet
both active and material participation tests) you will not
be allowed to claim net losses each year. But for most individuals who buy rental income properties or fixer-uppers, meeting these tests is not difficult. If you hire an
independent *property management company* the test of
active participation depends on how much involvement
you have. If you live out of town and delegate *all* decisions to the company, you probably will not meet the
active participation test. But if you continue to approve
tenants, set rent levels, approve repair expenses in advance, and decide when to sell properties, you are usually considered to meet the active participation test.

You are further limited as to how much you are allowed to deduct each year. No matter how many rental income properties you own, you are never allowed to deduct
more than $25,000 in annual net losses. This maximum
level will be reduced when your income is over $100,000.

When your net losses are higher than the allowable deduction, the excess has to be carried over and
used in the future. You will be allowed to deduct unused
losses in one of two ways. Either they can be deducted
when your overall losses do not exceed the maximum
you are allowed; or you can use net losses to reduce capital gains when you sell the rental income property. Because the property-specific loss is treated in this way, it
is essential that you keep careful records of expenses for
each property. When you own more than one rental income property, some expenses have to be treated as *allocated expenses* between properties.

Most expenses are easily identified by property.
Mortgage interest, property taxes, insurance, repairs and
utilities—your major expenses—are unique to each
property. Some expenses, like professional fees, office
supplies, and automobile expenses do not necessarily belong to any one property. You could simply divide these
expenses evenly; for example, if you own three properties, one-third of these expenses could be assigned to
each property. A more accurate method is to base alloca-
tions on the amount of rent.

material participation
a level of involve-
ment required to
qualify for deduc-
tion of net losses
from rental in-
come activity.
Individuals must
own at least 10
percent of a prop-
erty to qualify for
deduction of
annual net losses.

property management company
an independent
company special-
izing in managing
rental income
properties for
investors. They
advertise proper-
ties, screen ten-
ants, collect rents,
manage the prop-
erty bank account,
keep records, and
handle normal
maintenance (yard
work, periodic
repairs) as well as
unusual problems
(tenant or neigh-
bor complaints, for
example). The
level of control by
the company,
versus involve-
ment by the in-
vestor, may
determine whether
the individual
meets the active
participation test
for tax purposes.

allocated expenses
those expenses not directly attributable to any specific property, that are assigned to two or more properties (including professional fees, office supplies, and auto expenses, for example). The most consistent method for allocating expenses is on the basis of rents collected.

For example, you own three properties. Last year, you received rents as follows:

Property A	$6,750	52%
Property B	$4,200	32%
Property C	$2,150	16%
Total	$13,100	100%

Based on this breakdown, you would allocate expenses to each property on a percentage-of-rent basis. When you allocate, keep complete records so that you know how you calculated the breakdown in future periods.

When you sell properties, allocated expenses may become important if you have not been able to claim all of your annual net losses. The level of unclaimed loss will affect your capital gain on the sold property.

You can deduct up to $25,000 per year in rental income net losses. However, if your *adjusted gross income (AGI)* is higher than $100,000, the maximum loss is reduced by 50 cents for each dollar above that level. For example, if your adjusted gross income is $102,000, your maximum real estate losses are reduced by one-half of the excess $2,000, to $24,000 maximum. If your adjusted gross income is $120,000 your maximum loss is reduced to $15,000. And if your AGI is at or above, $150,000, you are not allowed to claim any rental income investment losses. Those losses have to be carried forward and used in future years, or applied against capital gains when you sell the property.

adjusted gross income (AGI)
for tax purposes, your total income after claiming adjustments for IRA, student loan interest, tuition, moving expenses, self-employment tax, alimony paid, and certain other items; and before calculating itemized or standard deduction or tax credits.

The calculation of adjusted gross income on your federal tax return is based on the line items on the form 1040. However, for calculating maximum real estate deductions allowed, the calculation is more complex. You need to figure out the *modified AGI* to determine your maximum allowable annual deduction. In this calculation, most adjustments are disallowed for a majority of people.

The distinction between AGI and modified AGI is important when your income is higher than $100,000 and could be important if (1) your income level is close to $100,000 and (2) your adjustments to gross income are high. For example, if your AGI is $95,000, but you have $9,000 in disallowed adjustments, you have to recalculate:

Adjusted gross income	$95,000
Plus disallowed adjustments	9,000
Modified AGI	$104,000
Maximum income level	100,000
Excess	$4,000
One-half of excess	$2,000

In the above calculation, it first appears that AGI is under $100,000. But modified AGI puts that level above the limit, so the $25,000 maximum deduction would be reduced to $23,000. If your net losses from rental income investments exceeded the $23,000 level, the excess would have to be carried forward as an unused loss.

Depreciation: The Basic Rules

Another area of tax law that you need to master is *depreciation*, the methods for claiming deductions for real estate over many years. Depreciation is a process by which expenses are spread over time rather than claimed all at once.

The terminology of depreciation is complex, but once mastered, it becomes apparent that the rules simply instruct you how to calculate annual deductions for various types of property. As a general rule, any property that has a *useful life* beyond one year has to be recognized as a capital asset and depreciated on a specific schedule.

The term is somewhat misleading. It implies that, at the expiration of the useful life, the asset has zero value. In one respect this is true; the *book value* of a capital asset is zero at the end of the depreciation period. However, in some instances, the real value does not necessarily decline. Autos and trucks do lose value over their useful lives, but real estate tends to increase in value. So the calculation is not designed to accurately reflect the tangible value of assets. It is more accurate to think of depreciation as an orderly process for recognizing a portion of the asset's cost each year until it reaches a book value of zero.

modified AGI
adjusted gross income excluding IRA contributions, student loan interest, taxable Social Security benefits, interest on student loans, self-employment tax, and tuition.

depreciation
a deduction for the value of capital assets, such as improvements to real estate, allowable over a period of years rather than in the year of purchase.

useful life
an approximation of the number of years a capital asset can be depreciated, based on the class of asset.

book value
the net value recorded after depreciation has been calculated. Once an asset has been fully depreciation, book value is zero, even if the asset continues to have market value.

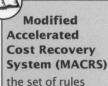

Modified Accelerated Cost Recovery System (MACRS)
the set of rules and restrictions concerning depreciation and how it has to be reported.

accelerated depreciation
a method of calculating depreciation in which a larger amount can be deducted in the early years of useful life, and less in later years. This system is allowed for autos and trucks, computers, and office equipment, but is not allowed for improvements to real estate, which have to be depreciated under the straight-line method.

straight-line depreciation
a method of computing depreciation in which the same amount is claimed each year throughout the useful life. Straight-line depreciation is required for real estate depreciation.

Depreciation is calculated for most assets using the *Modified Accelerated Cost Recovery System (MACRS)*, an extended name for what most people simply called "depreciation." MACRS is the outgrowth of many reforms and changes to the original tax code many years ago. Some assets can be written off using *accelerated depreciation* rates, while others, such as real estate, have to be depreciated using the *straight-line depreciation* method. The rules about which methods you are allowed to use are summarized in the following discussion.

The useful life of assets is expressed as the number of years over which it can be depreciated. The *recovery period* describes the various classes in which different types of property are classified. Many are designed for a very narrow range of assets; the recovery periods applicable to most investments in real estate are 5, 7, 27.5 and 31.5 year classifications:

5-year property includes autos and light trucks, office machinery and computers, as well as landscaping equipment and appliances.

7-year property includes office furniture.

27.5-year property includes residential real estate (defining for the purpose of depreciation as any building in which 80% or more of units are residential).

31.5 year property includes nonresidential real estate.

You are allowed to make certain *elections* under the tax rules. These are decisions to use different methods for calculating depreciation. Most elections are irrevocable and apply to all assets in a recovery period. As a matter of tax planning, you may elect to depreciate assets over a longer period than specified in the rules. This would make sense when your deductions exceed the maximum you are allowed to claim, for example. However, making elections is complex and could have consequences in future years. Before making depreciation elections, you should consult with your tax expert.

The methods used to calculate depreciation are based on the recovery period and on allowed accelerated or straight-line methods. You may also need to report *amortization* on the same form. This applies to any points that you are charged by a lender. These are usually amortized over the term of the loan. For example, if you borrow $100,000 and you are charged three points ($3,000), you are required to amortize that expense over the 30-year term. (If you replace the loan or sell the property before the 30 years, you claim the remaining balance of unamortized points, as a reduction to your capital gain.) In this example, you would report $100 per year as amortization.

The precise amount of depreciation you claim in the first year that you acquire an asset depends on the timing of your purchase and on the type of asset involved. The *mid-month convention* is a method for calculating the exact amount of deduction you are allowed during the first year you acquire residential real estate. The *half-year convention* applies to most other assets you may acquire, such as vehicles, office equipment, landscaping equipment or appliances.

The method of calculating the first-year depreciation for real estate is based on the percentages shown in Table 7.1.

These percentages are calculated based on the portion of the year remaining based on the month the asset was purchased. For example, if you purchased real estate in March (the third month), the mid-month calculation would allow depreciation for 19/24ths of the year. Assuming that the value of the building was $85,000, the calculation would be applied against that value each year. There are 24 mid-months every year, so depreciation would be calculated for (1) the remaining mid-month period, (2) the allowed 27.5-year depreciation period, and (3) the value of the asset:

(a) $19 \div 24 = .79167$

(b) $.79167 \div 27.5 = 2.879\%$

(c) $2.879\% \times \$85,000 = \$2,447.15$

recovery period
the class of assets, defining the number of years in the useful life, which mandates the calculation of depreciation and the method (accelerated or straight-line) that can be used.

elections
decisions to use depreciation methods other than the prescribed general methods. Elections are usually irrevocable and apply to all assets in a specific recovery period.

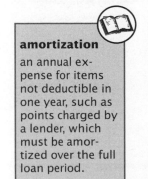

amortization
an annual expense for items not deductible in one year, such as points charged by a lender, which must be amortized over the full loan period.

Valuable Resource

To download a copy of specific instructions concerning depreciation, check the Internal Revenue Service Web site at http://www.irs.ustreas.gov, and print a copy of the publication *Instructions for Form 4562.*

mid-month convention

the method for calculating first-year depreciation for residential real estate. It is based on the month that the real estate purchase occurs.

The even-year and odd-year divisions vary to account for rounding, a distinction that may not affect most calculations, especially if you round to the closest dollar amount when you complete your tax return. However, the table is so precise because it applies uniformly, including single-family homes as well as multi-million-dollar real estate projects. So based on the year in service, a specific annual dollar amount is allowed. Using the same example as that show above, depreciation for the entire 27.5-year period is summarized in Table 7.2.

For property other than real estate, accelerated depreciation is allowed. The most common recovery periods are going to be five-year and seven-year classes. Table 7.3 summarizes the prescribed annual percentages allowed. For these classes of assets, the half-year convention is used.

half-year convention

the method for calculating first-year depreciation for assets used in conjunction with real estate other than the property itself; this includes most vehicles, office equipment, landscaping equipment and appliances.

This means that the calculations are based on the assumption that on average, assets were placed into service halfway through the year. For example, assuming an asset has a depreciable value of $4,000 and using the rate of 200 percent acceleration called for under the general depreciation system, the first-year would be calculated by first dividing the asset value by five (years); and then multiplying by the percentages supplied on the appropriate table. These tables are found in the IRS publication *Instructions for Form 4562* (see Valuable Resource on page 000) and also duplicated in the tables that appear in the rest of this chapter.

Under the alternative depreciation system, you can make an election to use 150 percent acceleration. In that case, the $4,000 asset would involve less depreciation in

TABLE 7.1 Mid-Month Convention for Real Estate

Month asset was placed in service	Years			
	1	2–9	Even	Odd
1	3.485%	3.636%	3.637%	3.636%
2	3.182	3.636	3.637	3.636
3	2.879	3.636	3.637	3.636
4	2.576	3.636	3.637	3.636
5	2.273	3.636	3.637	3.636
6	1.970	3.636	3.637	3.636
7	1.667	3.636	3.636	3.637
8	1.364	3.636	3.636	3.637
9	1.061	3.636	3.636	3.637
10	0.758	3.636	3.636	3.637
11	0.455	3.636	3.636	3.637
12	0.152	3.6356	3.636	3.637

TABLE 7.2 Example of a Mid-Month Convention: $85,000 Purchased in March

Year	Percentage	Amount	Year	Percentage	Amount
1	2.879%	$2,447.15	15	3.636%	$3,090.60
2	3.636	3,090.60	16	3.637	3,091.45
3	3.636	3,090.60	17	3.636	3,090.60
4	3.636	3,090.60	18	3.637	3,091.45
5	3.636	3,090.60	19	3.636	3,090.60
6	3.636	3,090.60	20	3.637	3,091.45
7	3.636	3,090.60	21	3.636	3,090.60
8	3.636%	$3,090.60	22	3.637%	$3,091.45
9	3.636	3,090.60	23	3.636	3,090.60
10	3.637	3,091.45	24	3.637	3,091.45
11	3.636	3,090.60	25	3.636	3,090.60
12	3.637	3,091.45	26	3.637	3,091.45
13	3.636	3,090.60	27	3.636	3,090.60
14	3.637	3,091.45	28	3.636	2,189.60
			Total	100.0%	$85,000.00

the first year, with the difference made up in future periods. Accelerated depreciation for five-year and for seven-year recovery periods under both of these methods, is summarized in Table 7.3.

In both instances of accelerated depreciation, the acceleration occurs during the first three to four years, and then levels out and reverts to straight-line depreciation for the remaining periods. The advance of acceleration is that it provides you a higher deduction in the early years. This may be very useful in calculating after-tax cash flow. However, if your real estate rental income losses exceed $25,000 per year, or if your modified AGI is above $100,000, it may be

TABLE 7.3   Example of a Half-Year Convention: $4,000 Asset

200% Accelerated Depreciation

	5-year Recovery Period			7-year Recovery Period	
Year	Percentage	Amount	Year	Percentage	Amount
1	20.00%	$ 800.00	1	14.29%	$ 571.60
2	32.00	1,280.00	2	24.49	979.60
3	19.20	768.00	3	17.49	699.60
4	11.52	460.80	4	12.49	449.60
5	11.52	460.80	5	8.93	357.20
6	5.76	230.40	6	8.92	356.80
			7	8.93	357.20
			8	4.46	178.40
Total	100.00	$4,000.00	Total	100.00	$4,000.00

150% Accelerated Depreciation

	5-year Recovery Period			7-year Recovery Period	
Year	Percentage	Amount	Year	Percentage	Amount
1	15.00%	$ 600.00	1	10.71%	$ 428.40
2	25.50	1,020.00	2	19.13	765.20
3	17.85	714.00	3	15.03	601.20
4	16.66	666.40	4	12.25	490.00
5	16.66	666.40	5	12.25	490.00
6	8.33	333.20	6	12.25	490.00
			7	12.25	490.00
			8	6.13	245.20
Total	100.00	$4,000.00	Total	100.00	$4,000.00

advantageous to elect to depreciate all assets using the straight-line method. Most depreciation-related elections have to be made for the first year in which depreciation is claimed, so you need to consult with your tax advisor before deciding whether elections are beneficial or not.

Two elections will be of interest to you. The first is the election to use 150 percent acceleration instead of 200 percent. You can make this election simply by writing 150 in the "Rate" column on Schedule 4562 (Depreciation). The second election is to use straight-line depreciation instead of accelerated depreciation. This election applies to *all* assets in the same recovery period each year and the election cannot be revoked later. To make this election, called an "IRC Section 168 election," you need to attach a brief statement to your tax return for the first year in which depreciation is claimed. The statement should read:

> I elect under Section 168(b)(5) to have provisions of Section 168(b)(3)(D) apply to all property placed in service in the tax year ended December 31, 20___, that was included as part of the _____-year recovery period.

You fill in the tax year and the recovery period. If you make the election to use straight-line depreciation, it is easy to compute. The half-year convention still applies. Referring to the previous example of a $4,000 asset, depreciation under this election would be computed as shown in Table 7.4.

The decision to use straight-line depreciation depends on the value of deductions today, versus your estimation of their value in the future. The greater the future need, the more you may want to defer claiming depreciation. If you think future tax rates will be higher, you may wish to make a straight-line election. If you really would prefer to take deductions sooner, use accelerated methods.

TABLE 7.4 Example of a Straight-Line Depreciation: $4,000 Asset

5-year Recovery Period			7-year Recovery Period		
Year	Percentage	Amount	Year	Percentage	Amount
1	10.00%	$ 400.00	1	7.13%	$ 285.20
2	20.00	800.00	2	14.29	571.60
3	20.00	800.00	3	14.29	571.60
4	20.00	800.00	4	14.29	571.60
5	20.00	800.00	5	14.29	571.60
6	10.00	400.00	6	14.29	571.60
			7	14.29	571.60
			8	7.13	285.20
Total	100.00	$4,000.00	Total	100.00	$4,000.00

Figuring the Base for Depreciation

The depreciation rules appear complex at first glance, but an analysis reveals that this area of calculation is not difficult to master. The tables for prescribed methods are provided in the depreciation instruction manual. Once you understand the purpose of depreciation and apply it to your real estate investment situation, you quickly gain control over this specialized area of tax law.

Some special rules do apply, however. For example, you are allowed to depreciate capital improvements such as buildings, additions, and major repairs. However, you cannot claim depreciation deductions for land. This raises the question: How do you calculate the value of land versus the value of improvements? Any number of possible methods is possible, but the three easiest ones are:

1. *Assessed value.* Your county charges property taxes based on assessed value of your property. This value often is the same as current market value, or it may be considerably lower, depending on location, state law, and frequency of assessment updates.

2. *Appraisal report.* You probably have an appraisal report from your lender, based on the appraisal completed at the time you purchased the property. This report estimates the current value of both land and improvements.

3. *Insurance value.* Your insurance carrier identifies the value of improvements to your property. Based on that value, you can identify land value as the difference between your purchase price and the amount being insured.

The method you pick to use in calculating depreciation should be based on what you want to achieve. If you want to be able to claim maximum depreciation, select the method that assigns the lowest value to land; this increases the portion of total value for improvements and, as a result, the amount of depreciation you can claim. However, if you do not need higher deductions, use a method that assigns a higher value to improvements.

Example of an Annual Depreciation Calculation

You purchased property and closed last month; the total purchase price was $125,000. You need to set up your books and records to separate land and improvements so that you can calculate annual depreciation. You have chosen the assessment value to break down these two segments. According to the latest tax bill, the county has based its assessment on a breakdown of $65,000 for improvements and $20,000 for land. (It is possible that these values will be updated following completion of the sale. Assessed value often lags behind current market value until property changes hands.)

To divide the total you paid, $125,000, between these two values, first determine the percentage based on assessed value:

Land	$20,000	23.5%
Improvements	$65,000	76.5
Total	$85,000	100.0%

Now apply this breakdown to your purchase price:

$$\text{Land, } 23.5\% \times \$125,000 = \$29,375$$

$$\text{Improvements, } 76.5\% \times \$125,000 = \$95,625$$

You can depreciate $95,625 using this method. The prescribed rate of 27.5 years will provide you with straight-line depreciation (after the first year) of $3,477 per year.

To document your method, write up a simple page showing the calculation and keep this with your tax records. In the event your calculation is questioned, you can provide your worksheet along with a copy of the tax assessment. The same applies if you base your breakdown on an appraisal or insurance report.

There are two types of depreciation worksheets you will need as part of preparation for your income tax return. Even if you start out with only one property, the recordkeeping is going to become complex as you add other assets (appliances, improvements, landscaping equipment, etc.). Both types of worksheets can be set up on a worksheet program such as Microsoft Excel.

The first is a depreciation worksheet that summarizes each year's calculation of depreciation. This may become a supplementary schedule that you will attach to your tax return. The depreciation form does not always provide enough space to show all of your calculations. For example, if you own more than one property, you will need to attach a worksheet showing how depreciation was calculated for each. Figure 7.1 shows a blank worksheet format that you can set up in Excel.

Depreciation Worksheet

Name _____ Social Security # _____ Year _____

Description of Property	Cost	Prior Depreciation	Method	Recovery Years	Rate	Recovery Years
Total						

FIGURE 7.1 Depreciation worksheet.

On this worksheet, each asset (building, other improvement, auto, etc.) is listed separately; and the totals are carried over to the tax form. The "Cost" column is your depreciable basis, such as the value of building excluding land. In subsequent years, the sum of all prior years' depreciation is listed in the third column. The next three columns define the type of depreciation you are claiming. For various types of assets, these three columns would reflect different forms of information. For example, in the second year, the information could show:

	Method	*Years*	*Recovery Rate*
Building	SL	27.5	3.636%
Computer	200 DB	5	32%

Under the "Method" column, SL stands for straight-line and 200 DB translates to the declining balance method at a 200% rate. Refer back to Tables 7.2 and 7.3 to find the rates shown above.

The second worksheet is a summary of depreciation you will claim for the full recovery period of each asset. This is a worksheet you can set up going left to right or top to bottom, depending on your personal preferences. Programs such as Excel are very useful for this purpose. Table 7.5 shows one example of a top-to-bottom method for a building, a computer, and office furniture.

TABLE 7.5   Example of a Worksheet Showing Top-to-Bottom Depreciation Method

	Building, 113 Harbor Street: $95,625 2/15/05 - SL, 27.5 years	Computer System: 8/12/05, $1,215 200 DB, 5 years	Office Furniture: 6/1/05, $462 200 DB 7 years	
Tax Year				Total
2005				
Rate	3.182%	20.00%	14.20%	
Prior	0	0	0	$ 0
Depreciation	$3,043	$243	$66	3,352
2006				
Rate	3.636	32.00	24.49	
Prior	$3,043	$243	$66	$ 3,352
Depreciation	$3,477	$389	$113	3,979
2007				
Rate	3.636	19.20	17.49	
Prior	$6,520	$632	$179	$ 7,331
Depreciation	$3,477	$233	$81	3,791
2008				
Rate	3.636	11.52	12.49	
Prior	$9,997	$865	$260	$11,122
Depreciation	$3,477	$140	$58	3,675
2009				
Rate	3.636	11.52	8.93	
Prior	$13,474	$1,005	$318	$14,797
Depreciation	$3,477	$140	$41	3,658
2010				
Rate	3.636	5.76	8.92	
Prior	$16,951	$1,145	$359	$18,455
Depreciation	$3,477	$70	$41	3,588
2011				
Rate	3.636	—	8.93	
Prior	$20,428	$1,215	$400	$22,043
Depreciation	$3,477	0	$41	3,518
2012				
Rate	3.636	—	4.46	
Prior	$23,905	$1,215	$441	$25,561
Depreciation	$3,477	0	$21	3,498

The format can be carried through to the extent required; for example, for real estate, you would need to proceed through to the end of the 28th year. Each year's prior depreciation is carried forward, and increased by the depreciation claimed for the previous year. This worksheet provides all of the information needed to fill in the form shown in Figure 7.1, for each tax year. Without a permanent record such as this, it can be tedious and time-consuming to reconstruct the calculation. The worksheet can also be expanded as new assets are added or as old ones are fully depreciated.

The worksheet becomes useful if you sell property before depreciation has been completed. Upon sale, the recapture rule comes into play. To calculate the capital gain, the adjusted basis is reduced to the extent of depreciation that has been claimed. Referring back to the example, we can assume that the purchase price was $125,000 ($95,625 building plus $29,375 land). We can also assume buyer's closing costs of $2,645. If this property were sold at the end of the eighth year (last row on Table 7.5) for $182,500 and with closing costs of $17,440, the calculation of the net capital gain would be:

Sales price	$182,500
Less seller's closing costs	17,440
Net sales price	$165,060
Basis:	
Purchase price	$125,000
Buyer's closing costs	2,645
Adjusted purchase price	$127,645
Less depreciation	–27,382
Adjusted basis	100,263
Capital gain	$64,797

In this example, the capital gain is calculated to included adjusted purchase and sale prices, and then increased by depreciation. This recapture increases the gain and, as a result, the tax that is due upon sale.

If you report a loss on the sale of real estate, you are limited to a maximum loss deduction of $3,000 per year. This includes *all* capital gains and losses. Therefore, if you report a real estate loss at the same time as profits from other investments, the $3,000 limitation refers to the net total. Thus, the timing of sales, not only of real estate, but other assets as well such as stocks, can make a big difference in your overall tax liability.

An interest tax planning idea involves conversion of a rental income property, to your primary residence. The tax rules state that you can sell your primary residence and escape tax on the first $500,000 profit (for a married couple) or $250,000 (for single people). In the example above, what would happen if instead of selling the property, you gave notice to your tenants, and moved into it? As long as you lived there at least two years out of the five-year period before the same, you could sell under the primary residence rule. In that situation, you would be required to pay tax on depreciation recapture, but not on the rest of the capital gain. So your taxable gain would be $27,382 instead of $64,797. That represents a big difference and the resulting lower income tax could make the conversion strategy worthwhile.

Tax-Deferred Exchanges

Another way you can reduce your tax liability is by *tax deferral* methods. This is any strategy that moves a tax liability to a later year. In the case of real estate investment property, you can defer profits indefinitely by going through a *like-kind exchange* of property, also called a *1031 exchange*.

> **tax deferral**
> any decisions made to avoid paying more taxes this year, by moving tax liabilities to future years.

The like-kind exchange rules are prescribed in Internal Revenue Code Section 1031. The rules can be complex, but to summarize, you need to meet these criteria to defer taxes on investment property:

1. Both original and investment properties must be investment real estate. (However, you can exchange one type of real estate for another and still qualify.)

2. The entire transaction has to be completed within 180 dates from the date of sale of the original property.

3. The purchase price of the replacement property has to be higher than the sales price of the first property.

4. The exchange of funds has to be handled through an independent facilitator.

5. The seller of the replacement property has to agree, in writing, to cooperate with you in the like-kind exchange.

> **like-kind exchange (1031 exchange)**
> in tax law, the replacement of one property with another of the same general classification. A like-kind exchange, properly executed, creates a deferral of tax liabilities until the replacement property is sold.

The rules are complex and you may need help completing all of the requirements.

Valuable Resource

To get a complete copy of IRC Section 1031, check the Web page at http://assembler.law.cornell.edu/uscode/html/uscode26/usc_sec_26 _00001031———000-.html. You can also find instructions and forms at the IRS website, http://www.irs.gov/. Download *Form 8824:, Like-Kind Exchanges,* and *Publication 544, Sales and Other Dispositions of Assets.* Like-kind exchanges are reported on Form 8824.

If you sell property through a like-kind exchange, you do not escape the tax liability. You defer it. Returning to the previous example, assume that you sold the property under a like-kind exchange. The profit of $64,797 would be deferred as long as you purchased a replacement property costing more than the sales price of $182,500. For example, say you found a replacement property for $195,000. In that situation, the basis of the new property is reduced by the amount of deferred gain:

Purchase price	$195,000
Less deferred gain	–64,797
Adjusted basis	$130,203

In this example, the newly acquired property's basis is reduced by the deferred gain; so when it is eventually sold, you would adjust not only for closing costs and add back depreciation. You would also be paying taxes on a wider margin because of this deferral.

The tax rules for rental income property are complex. You need to master the rules of depreciation and strategies for tax-deferral. You also need to be able to plan ahead and to consult with your tax expert on matters of tax planning. Investing in rental income property will complicate your tax return, but the special tax benefits make it worthwhile—even if you cannot deduct all of your losses.

For example, if you structure your investments so that you achieve a breakeven between rental income and deductions, you can still enjoy the tax benefits, but not through taking losses on your tax return. Instead, rents cover your mortgage payment, but depreciation helps you to avoid income taxes on your rents. For many, the tax benefits—capped as they are to $25,000 or less per year—represent only one form of benefit. The offset between income and deductions, plus breakeven cash flow, makes real estate a viable method for accumulating equity over many years.

The next chapter examines the nature of *risk* in rental income investing and offers guidelines for evaluating and comparing real estate to decide whether risks justify the potential profits.

Chapter

Risky Business and Rewarding Business
Comparisons

Risk is the most overlooked aspect of rental income investing. Considering the level of capital commitment, cash flow, and other important attributes, you will improve your chances of success by studying risk in its many forms—not to conclude that rental income investing is too risky to proceed, but only to ensure that you are aware of the potential dangers. On the contrary, the positive attributes and benefits of rental income investing are highly attractive; but smart investors know the whole range of risk/reward possibilities.

In the stock market, the dangers of potential losses are constantly on the minds of everyone, at least in one form: market risk. Stock investors continually monitor their investments, concerned that values will fall rather than rise. The highly liquid stock market is characterized by price gyrations, often across a broad spectrum of stocks, often moving illogically as well. Real estate contains the same risks, but not on a day-to-day basis. In fact, real estate risks should be taken just as seriously as stock market risks, but they often are not. The tendency is to consider real estate as the ultimate safe investment, and to view the potential for capital safety with positive cash flow, while perhaps overlooking or underestimating potential risks. However, even when you set up the investment to ensure the best possible outcome, that does not make the risks disappear.

Most people will agree with the following general observations:

1. You are always wise to know the risks of any investment before you begin.

2. Capital should be invested only when you are willing to accept the risks involved.

3. It is wiser to cut losses before they worsen; negative cash flow, for example, may represent a very real loss when the dollar amount exceeds probable rises in market value.

4. If you are dissatisfied with an investment, you are smart to get out. For example, if you discover that you do not enjoy dealing directly with tenants, you may find a property manager or you may want to simply sell the property and put your capital elsewhere.

5. Every investment, no matter how profitable, contains both positive and negative attributes. You cannot separate the two. The greater the opportunity for profit, the more risk you are likely to experience; and the safer your capital, the lower your expectations should be concerning future profits.

The Nature of Risk

The great irony for all investors is the tendency to consider only one half of the overall investment equation. Everyone gets excited about profit potential and perhaps even distracted by it, and may easily forget to also ask important questions about risk. It makes sense to come to an understanding of the nature of risk itself.

Risk and profit opportunity are really an equation. As one side changes, so must the other. Once you recognize that risk and opportunity rise and fall in unison, it becomes clear that *all* investments contain the same interaction. With stocks, risk is normally associated solely with price. Some stocks are more volatile than others; they represent greater profit potential as well as greater risk. Other stocks trade within a narrow price range but rise gradually in price over many years. These stocks return a relatively low percentage of profit, but also represent very low risk.

In real estate, the same interaction occurs, but it is less visible. This is because investors are accustomed to thinking in terms of price alone when the subject of risk comes up. Real estate has historically increased in value (based on national averages). And while price trends vary by region, it is fairly easy to spot areas where prices are on the rise. So picking the right area in which to invest in real estate is not difficult. Price—meaning the market price and, thus, market risk—in real estate is easier to identify than it is in the stock market, where a company's fortunes can change in a matter of hours. There is a tendency to ignore the other forms of risk involved with rental income investing, because market risk is easily quantified.

That basic form of risk itself is often downplayed because—again citing the averages—everyone knows that well-selected real estate rises in value over time, usually beating inflation. This makes real estate a "safe" investment. Many other advantages—the ability to insure the property, cash flow from tenant rents, and significant tax advantages—all augment the argument that real estate is a low-risk investment.

Risk, however, is usually based on the fact that we cannot see the future. A single incident can drastically affect real estate values and change long-term prospects for growth overnight. An extreme real estate example makes this point: The partial nuclear meltdown at Three Mile Island, Pennsylvania, on March 29, 1979, led to the evacuation of 140,000 people and an estimated $110 million in reduced property values.[1] It was not until 1999 that the nuclear property was sold; and even then it went for $99 million, less than one-fifth of its $512 million book value. This disaster, entirely unrelated to any of the normal criteria for picking properties or managing risks, demonstrates that any investment can fail. Anyone who invested in real estate in the central Pennsylvania area in 1979 suffered losses to their health, lifestyle, and investment value.

There are no guarantees that real estate you pick in even the strongest market will continue to rise in value in the future. If a major local employer decides to close down and relocate, that will reduce property values. An environmental problem could scare off buyers. A natural disaster such as an earthquake, hurricane, or flood will also have a devastating effect on property values.

Market risk, with these potential problems in mind, is ever present, not just in the rental income market, but in every market. There is no area of the country where you can ensure absolute safety for your real estate investment. Market value is going to be affected by changes from many sources, some predictable and others beyond anyone's control. A comforting point worth remembering is that everyone needs to live somewhere, so the attribute of real estate as a basic necessity ensures that value will hold over the long term. In fact, it is impossible to find an investment that will enable you to avoid risk altogether. The point here is that with real estate, you do not escape market risk. It is a reality. However, the better your analysis is in picking real estate, the better your chances for a successful experience; and the better you understand risk, the better prepared you are when markets slow down.

Comparative Risk Analysis

We know that market risk is beyond our control. We can control the market to a degree in the selection of investment products—stocks, mutual funds, real estate, etc. So given the fact that the unknown and unexpected loss can occur anywhere, we cannot avoid *all* risks; we have to concentrate on picking viable investments based on what we can control. This is where the art of studying comparative risks becomes valuable.

Everyone desires to have personal control over investment capital. At the same time, many desire the seemingly contradictory desire for professional guidance, and want to find someone to make decisions for them. This is why so many people invest in mutual funds. These investors believe that by picking a high-performing fund, they can depend on professional management to make the right decisions based on their expertise. This works for many people who want and need a degree of control, but do not want to make decisions concerning market risk and other forms of risk. In fact, the diversification achieved by placing a limited amount of money into a mutual fund is one of the fund's greatest safety features. The theory is that by purchasing shares of many diverse stocks, the mutual fund is a safer choice than buying individual stocks on your own. Sometimes this works, and sometimes it does not. Comparative risk is a process consisting of several stages:

1. *Personal control.* The starting point in comparative risk analysis is to ask yourself how much personal control you want with your investments. The extremely conservative investor will give up all personal control and invest cash in insured savings accounts or certificates of deposit. The market risk is very low, but so is the potential for profits. The speculator, in comparison, requires total control and seeks exceptional yields—and for that level of potential profit, he or she accepts exceptionally high risks. A day trader or options and commodities speculator may realize double-digit returns or lose everything, for example.

   With real estate, you have a good mixture of personal control with moderate risks. You insure the property against most types of known losses; you manage the property directly through selection of tenants, on-going maintenance, and neighborhood selection; and you decide how much rent to charge and when to buy or sell. However, even with this level of personal control, you are not involved in a high-risk venture; you are not speculating on volatile commodities. Real estate prices tend to move more gradually, so the volatility of market risk is lower as well.

2. *Risk/reward comparisons.* Once you define how much personal control you find desirable, you next will want to think about the relationship between risk and reward (profit). You have to contend with market risk, but that is only the beginning. The possibility that your property's market value could level out or even fall is worrisome, but as long as rent is covering your mortgage payments and other obligations, you can afford to wait for the real estate cycle to change directions. But you also need to be aware of the supply and demand market for rental

units, which is not the same as the residential housing market. Tenant supply and demand may vary seasonally or change because a lot of rental units are being constructed in the same city. Demand also varies with migratory population changes. People follow jobs so if employers are closing down in one area and moving to another, demand for real estate will follow the employment trend. Demand affects the market, and so does the supply. Market rates are affected when the supply of rental units rises. As your costs increase, you may have to raise rents to cover cash flow, which in turn increases the possibility for vacancies and poorer cash flow.

You also have to think about the potential for change in the market for financing. If you own investment property financed with a variable rate loan, your monthly payment will increase as market interest rates rise. Even in a loan that contains annual and lifetime *rate caps*, the possibility of higher mortgage payments is the risk attribute of the variable-rate mortgage.

> **rate cap**
> in a variable rate mortgage, contractual terms limiting how much interest rate increases are allowed. Two forms of cap are normally involved: (1) an annual limitation expressed in the number of interest points and (2) a lifetime cap defining the maximum rate a lender is allowed to charge.

3. *Attribute analysis.* Every investment contains specific attributes for leverage, liquidity, and diversification. These attributes define levels of risk. Real estate requires high leverage for most people because few have enough cash to buy properties outright. So you may leverage 70 to 80 percent of the rental income properties you buy. The high leverage translates to high risk. In fact, leverage risk is one of the most serious forms of risk you face when you invest in rental income properties. A period of vacancies or unexpected repairs could affect your ability to meet obligations every month, perhaps even requiring you to sell at a loss. In a severe negative cash flow situation, your personal credit could be affected as well. So leverage risk is, in many respects, a more serious concern than market risk.

Real estate investments also are not as liquid as savings accounts or the stock market. So *illiquidity* is an attribute of real estate that has to be viewed in context. You would not want to tie up an excessive amount of your total capital in illiquid investments; and with real estate, the only way to get capital out of the investment is to refinance or sell. This feature makes the point that you need to allocate some portion of your overall capital to more liquid investments, in case you need funds on short notice.

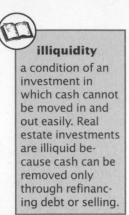

illiquidity

a condition of an investment in which cash cannot be moved in and out easily. Real estate investments are illiquid because cash can be removed only through refinancing debt or selling.

The third major attribute to remember is diversification. Unless you purchase several rental income properties, you cannot diversify by area, type of property or price. When you own a large number of properties, after-tax cash flow becomes more difficult due to the limitations on how much you can claim as a tax loss each year. So for any rental income property investor, diversification is achieved by spreading capital among several different markets; many refer to this form of diversification as asset allocation. For example, if you have $100,000 to invest, you may use $30,000 as a down payment on a rental income or fixer-upper property; place $20,000 in liquid savings or certificates of deposit; and invest the remaining $50,000 in mutual funds and directly owned stock.

4. *Availability of capital.* Some investment programs can be entered for very little money. Many no-load mutual funds will let you open an account for $100 and your local bank may sell you a certificate of deposit for a small amount as well. You can even buy single shares of stock if you are willing to pay a higher than average transaction fee. With real estate, however, you usually are required to make a down payment. Although owner-occupied primary residences can be financed at 90 percent (or even at 100 percent in some programs), lenders require a larger down payment for investment properties. A 30 percent down payment is typical and, while you may be able to find lenders with more liberal requirements, you still need to meet the ratios between income and debt to get approval for a loan. So the amount of capital you have available defines your ability to enter different types of investment programs and, in the case of real estate, also places a financial limit on how many properties you can afford to own. Your financial situation will also limit the scope of a real estate investment program, due to lender requirements.

5. *Cash flow planning.* The final attribute to consider is cash flow. Most types of investments do not create cash flow issues. For example, when you invest in a certificate of deposit or a mutual fund, you do not need to make periodic payments of any kind. You can simply invest money whenever it is available. With real estate, however, cash flow is often more important than long-term profits. For most people, the requirement for positive cash flow or, at the very least, breakeven levels, *is* the real bottom line. So the status of cash flow—and the possibility of vacancies and unexpected repairs—represents a serious risk.

Features Defining Risk

Risk is not a simple concept, and it cannot be defined based on a specific investment. Among the features that define risk is its uncertain borders. For example, if your investment capital is only a few thousand dollars, a risk defined as moderate may be beyond what you can afford exposure to; but if you have hundreds of thousands of dollars to invest, your attitude toward that same risk will be far different. Your *risk tolerance*—your ability and willingness to accept specific levels of risk—is a variable based on available capital, income, investing experience, and even your personality (you may be very conservative at heart, or you may be a high roller, for example). Today's risk tolerance level will change with major life events: marriage, birth of a child, losing your job, a career change, divorce, health problems, or the death of a family member.

risk tolerance
the level of risk an individual is willing and able to take with capital, based on personal income, family situation, and investing experience.

Risk is different for each individual. Even if it could be exactly defined in every case, a specific form of risk can take on a different look when the amount of capital changes. For example, if you own a single property and your rent is at 115% of your mortgage payment, the cash flow risk can be specifically defined. Vacancies, higher interest rates on your variance mortgage, unexpected repairs, and increases in insurance premiums or property taxes erode the margin of positive cash flow. The risk is specific to the one property. However, if you duplicate the same *level* of risk with three properties, you face a higher potential problem. The ratios remain the same and nothing has changed in the nature of the risk itself. But you have more capital at risk and potentially, you would face larger cash flow problems if all three properties faced unexpected expenses or vacancies. A counter-argument to this observation is that by diversifying capital among different properties, you reduce risk. This is only partially true.

Consider the case of diversifying by buying many different stocks. A market-wide correction is likely to cause price declines in most listed stocks, even those with strong fundamentals. Stock investors understand that to manage this potential problem, they need to invest outside of the stock market. In real estate, the same market forces may be at work. If market prices in your area soften, level out or decline, you will not experience the rate of growth you might have seen last year. If a developer builds an apartment complex, tenant demand will fall, creating the prospect of a higher vacancy rate. If you have variable rate mortgages on all of your rental income properties, a general increase in interest rates will lead to higher debt service, also affecting cash flow on all of your properties. So when more capital is at stake, your risk also increases.

Every rental income property investor has to be concerned with cash flow risk. Whether you flip properties as quickly as possible or hold properties for the long term, you constantly struggle to maintain the dynamic relationship between cash flow and profits. If you purchase properties with the understanding that real estate values increase over time, the assumption is accurate but incomplete. It may be true that over a period of many years your investments will be profitable; but you also need to be able to afford to keep ahead of your expenses. It is easy to get into a situation in which changes in market value are not keeping pace with your net cash outlay. For example, paying interest over many years raises questions about whether rental income property is profitable over the long term. Because the cost of borrowing is so high, interest payments over many years inhibit your overall profits. Because property values rise, it remains likely that you will be able to profit from buying rental income properties. But the risk remains: If your property does not increase in value, the potential for profits is reduced. Your rental income may cover your cash flow; but you need growth in market value to justify the investment.

In the classic explanation of why rental income property makes sense, the argument states that "tenants pay your mortgage" for you. The basic cash flow equation does, in fact, assume that rents will be adequate to cover mortgage payments. However, if you calculate your after-tax cash flow and conclude that you are at a breakeven level, what happens if other expenses arise? The essential question at that point becomes: Is the increase in market value of the property keeping pace with or exceeding the annual outlay of cash? Another important question may be: Considering the marginal advantages of owning this property, is it justified by the corresponding risk?

Some investors believe it is acceptable to live with after-tax negative cash flow because (1) it is minimal, (2) the situation is not necessarily permanent, and (3) market values are going to outpace the cash outlay over the long term. If all of those assumptions are true, then it makes perfect sense to wait out a soft market. If you can afford temporary or minimal negative cash flow, and if you accept that as a feature you can live with, then the net cash outlay can be viewed as a part of your long-term plan. What makes a risk unacceptable is when negative cash flow places a burden on your personal budget, and when you do not see any prospect for turning the venture into a profitable scenario.

The arguments favoring rental income property investing might all be true. But while long-term property values may increase, what if real estate values in your region level out over the next five years? If values do not increase, that means that any after-tax negative cash flow represents a loss. If you sell your property without recapturing that loss, the entire investment loses, too. You need to experience enough growth in market value to outpace negative cash flow, *and* to cover closing costs on both sides of the transaction. If you realize that you will be lucky just to break even, why invest in the first place? As with any investment, the assumptions have to be realistic and the numbers have to work out.

Analysis of potential problems can be performed on a comparative basis. For example, assume that you can afford to make a $30,000 down payment on a $100,000 house. Your 30-year loan on $70,000 at 6.5 percent will cost $442.45 per month. Market rents are about $500. However, you also have to pay part of the utilities, the property taxes, and the insurance. Added together, you expect to experience a breakeven before taxes, and you estimate an annual reserve of about $500 for repairs and maintenance. If your assumptions are right and the market value increases by 4 percent per year, the property will be worth $116,986 after four years.

$$\$100,000 \times (1.04)^4 = \$116,986$$

Next, assume that closing costs on purchase and sale add up to $12,000. That reduces your net profit to about $4,986 over the four-year period. If you had invested your $30,000 at 3 percent in an insured account instead of buying real estate, your return would be $2,782:

$$\$30,000 \times (1.03)^4 = \$32,782$$

Buying real estate in this case would yield $4,986 based on your estimates; placing the same down payment amount in a 3 percent investment would yield $2,782, or about $2,204 less. However, there is another problem: These return calculations are very dissimilar in several ways:

1. *Cash flow risk only exists on one side of the comparison.* There is no debt service with a savings account. The existence of debt service in real estate makes this investment a higher risk with a potentially higher profit over the long term.

2. *Outcomes are estimated in one case and ensured in the other.* You estimate your property value cash flow and market value outcomes, but you have no way of knowing how the picture will evolve. In comparison, you can lock in a rate with certificates of deposit. (You can also find stocks yielding 3 percent or more each year.)

3. *The amount of work you will need to perform is dissimilar.* Rental income property investing requires your time and effort in addition to money. Even if your involvement is limited to monitoring tenants and taking care of periodic repairs, it remains a commitment, With a savings account, you can just deposit your cash and forget it.

4. *Liquidity is vastly different between these investment choices.* With real estate, you can only get cash out by selling or refinancing. With a savings account you can withdraw all or part of your money whenever you want. If you buy a product with a guaranteed rate of interest, there may be a penalty if you withdraw funds before a specified date; but even with this limitation, savings provide far more liquidity.

These points do not mean it is a poor idea to invest in real estate. The possibility has to be considered, though, that buying rental income property could be less advantageous than other choices. The point here is that the bleak prospect should be considered; risk analysis requires that you consider a range of possible outcomes. On the other side of the spectrum, real estate values may rise dramatically so that you could triple your down payment investment in only a few years; your tenants may be exceptional and pay rent on time without ever disturbing you; and you never experience an unexpected repair.

A range of possibilities makes your analysis more complete. If you want to evaluate and compare different investments realistically, you will also accept the risk/reward equation as part of the whole picture. Real estate values tend to hold up well and to increase steadily; properties are insured; and you have maximum personal control. But you have to contend with market forces beyond your control, as well as with tenants, the possibility of negative cash flow, and other risks. The potential risks are offset by the potential rewards.

Another form of risk you need to think about with real estate, is personal credit risk. This is the risk that cash flow will become negative to the point that you would not be able to keep up with monthly mortgage payments. This would affect your credit rating. Most real estate investors depend on excellent credit to get the best financing terms, and with any negative points on your credit report, that becomes difficult. Even people with mediocre credit can find financing for their primary residence, but that is much more difficult for investment properties.

Tax and Inflation Risks

Risk comes in many forms. We have talked about tax benefits throughout this book, but in real estate you also face a tax *risk*. This is true for all investments, of course. You are taxed on your profits, so some of your profits go to the government. If you report a net loss on your tax return from real estate activities, the tax benefits can make a difference between positive and negative cash flow. However, if you report a net profit, the tax liability reduces your cash flow.

Another form of tax risk is the added complexity of your tax return. Typically, real estate investors have to file at least two additional forms each year.

Valuable Resource

Check the CPI homepage at the U.S. Bureau of Labor Statistics Web site, http://www.bls.gov/cpi/home.htm—There you will find an explanation for how CPI is computed and the latest statistics.

Schedule E is used to summarize rental income activity, and *Form 4562* is required for reporting depreciation. Beyond this, when you sell property, you need special forms to report capital gains or, if applicable, like-kind exchanges. The added complexity also affects your calculation of a maximum allowable annual deduction based on your gross income. So for many people who have enjoyed filing a simple, straightforward tax return each year, real estate moves the whole reporting scenario to a much more complex level.

> **Consumer Price Index (CPI)**
> the best-known measurement of inflation, an index developed to measure changes in prices from one year to the next, in many categories. The CPI indicates the health of the economy, especially in major markets, including housing prices.

A related risk all investors face is inflation. In recent years, the inflation rate as measured by the *Consumer Price Index (CPI)* has been low and, on average, real estate values have exceeded the rate of inflation. So even with a low inflation rate, real estate has served historically as an effective hedge against inflation risk.

When you consider the effects of inflation and taxes together, you realize that with any investment, the after-tax, after-inflation *net breakeven point* is not the same as the simple rate of return. To calculate net breakeven point, you need to divide the rate of inflation by your net after-tax rate of income. With I representing the rate of inflation, T your effective income tax rate and B your required net breakeven point, the formula is:

$$I \div 100 - T = B$$

The effective tax rate should include your combined federal and state taxes. For example, if you are paying 28 percent as an effective federal tax rate, and another 10 percent in state taxes, your effective rate, overall, is 38 percent. That would leave an after-tax income rate of 62 percent.

> **net breakeven point**
> the rate of return you need when considering the effects of inflation and income taxes. To be completely accurate, the effective tax rate should include both federal and state tax rates.

Valuable Resource

To view state taxes for each state, check the Web site http://www.tax-admin.org/fta/rate/ind_inc.html. This site reports current tax rates for every state, including which types of income are taxed.

TABLE 8.1   Net Breakeven Point

Tax Bracket*	Inflation Rate				
	1%	2%	3%	4%	5%
15	1.18%	2.35%	3.53%	4.71%	5.88%
20	1.25	2.50	3.75	5.00	6.25
25	1.33	2.67	4.00	5.33	6.67
30	1.43	2.86	4.29	5.71	7.14
35	1.54	3.08	4.62	6.15	7.69
40	1.67	3.33	5.00	6.67	8.33
45	1.82	3.64	5.45	7.27	9.09
50	2.00	4.00	6.00	8.00	10.00

*Combined federal and state.

The calculation of net breakeven point is shown in the chart on Table 8.1

Mortgage Cost Risk

A final form of risk every rental income property investor faces is mortgage cost risk. In its most obvious form, the risk is easy to evaluate. A variable-rate mortgage may increase up to a specified annual cap, and up to a lifetime cap rate as well. By studying amortization tables, you can assess the risk of higher monthly payments. For example, if your current rate on a $70,000, 30-year loan is 6.5 percent, your monthly payment is $442.45. If the variable rate were to increase to 8.5 percent, the payment would be $536.24, or $93.79 more per month. (This increase is based on the assumption that the outstanding loan balance would be identical; actual increase may be lower if the remaining loan balance was lower as well.)

The risk of increasing mortgage payments is only the visible form of mortgage risk. A far greater risk is that, over many years, interest payments will erode market value. In that case, the lender would make all of the money, and you as an investor would be fortunate to break even—assuming that property values remained the same. In reality, many property values have increased dramatically in recent years so, assuming that trend continues, most real estate investors are not concerned with the cost of borrowing; they depend on long-term growth in market value. The mortgage risk is applicable to your primary residence more than to investment properties; typically, you will pay for your home two and half times if you count 30-year interest expense as part of the cost of buying. However, when you rent out investment property, you also assume that you cover your mortgage costs with rental income. For that reason, it makes sense that you may not be as concerned with the true cost of property as you are on your primary residence. Even so, the numbers are staggering when you consider the long-term interest cost.

For example, if your $70,000 loan is amortized over 30 years at 6.5 percent, your true overall cost is $159,282, meaning your $70,000 loan will cost $89,282 in interest. If you cannot cover the entire cost of debt service with rent, you may need to evaluate the after-tax cash flow based on selling your property at various times. Few investors plan to keep their rental income properties for 30 years. If you plan to sell within five or 10 years, you may be unable to make a profit on the transaction. Again, based on a 30-year amortization at 6.5 percent, after five years you will have paid off only about $4,473. The total payments of $26,547 would consist of $22,074 in interest. If you were to sell after 10 years, you will have paid off only $16,906 out of a total of $53,094 in payments. Even on an after-tax basis, these numbers reveal that buying property and financing most of the purchase price means you pay more for the investment than the stated purchase price.

These realities are not a problem as long as (1) rents are consistently paid so that your mortgage obligation is, indeed, covered; (2) property values increase adequately to create an acceptable *realistic* rate of return; and (3) you experience no expensive surprise repairs.

With the 10-year example, if you accept the argument that "tenants pay your mortgage" for you (again, assuming you have no vacancies over the 10-year period), you will have saved $16,906 through periodic payments to principal. Using that figure as a base, you would next want to calculate the likely profit on the property, based on average annual growth in market value, closing costs, taxes, and your time and effort.

Real estate investment has proven to be one of the safest and most profitable alternatives available. But before proceeding, some comparative analysis of all possible outcomes, including the worst-case scenario, is advisable. Remembering that comparisons between different markets are not made on a true like-kind basis, you can still make an informed decision about how and where to invest. When you remember the differences in cash flow, liquidity, tax benefits, and the amount of capital involved, you can assess the relative potential and risk of different investment choices. The more informed you are about the possibility of loss based on various risks you accept when you buy rental income property, the better equipped you are to manage those risks. The same is true for any form of investing. Stock market investors need to analyze financial statements, and should not rely on rumors and tips from friends. Speculators should be fully aware of the potential for loss as well as the potential for profit. And real estate investors need to be aware of the importance of cash flow and market risk, as well as using realistic numbers in their comparative analysis.

The next chapter focuses on another aspect of investment and risk management, the need for long-term planning through diversification and asset allocation.

Chapter

Diversification and Allocation
Many Baskets and Many Eggs

The concept of diversification is widely misunderstood. This is true in the stock market, as well as in real estate and other forms of investing. Many believe that simply by spreading capital among several different products (such as stocks) they achieve a diversified portfolio. This is not always true.

The need for diversification is fairly easy to meet in the stock market because the unit price of shares is fairly low. You can buy many different stocks, even with a limited amount of capital, and achieve some degree of diversification. For real estate investors, the problem is quite different. Many rental income property owners simply cannot afford to buy many properties in different areas, so they cannot diversify their real estate holdings. They have to accept an undiversified form of risk.

The desire for diversification may also contradict other goals. For example, most books written for landlords advise that rental properties should be purchased close to where you live. This enables you to keep an eye on tenants. You also know the market. So there are practical reasons to limit your investments geographically. However, this practical limitation also prevents you from diversifying your rental income holdings. It is likely that economic trends, either positive or negative, affect an entire region. Employment, building trends, and interest rates have a broad effect on properties within a single county or even your entire state. For this reason, there may be a conflict between the desirability of limiting your geographic market and the general wisdom of diversifying how you invest your capital.

The Purpose for Diversification

Most real estate books have no discussion of diversification. The topic is primarily associated with the stock market or, in a broader sense, with financial planning as a long-term application. However, spreading risks—which is the purpose behind diversification—is just as important to rental income investors as it is to stock investors.

All investors need to spread risks in appropriate and practical ways. The popularity of mutual funds makes this point. For very little initial capital, you can own small partial shares in dozens of stocks, all selected by professional managers. While this form of diversification is not perfect, it achieves more than trying to achieve the same thing by buying stocks directly. The mutual fund concept enables investors to diversify even a small amount of capital.

Real estate investors cannot diversify within the real estate market as easily. As a rental income property owner, you want to protect yourself against well-known risks: market, tenant, cash flow, liquidity, and interest rate risks are the best known among these. The theory of diversification tells us that by buying dissimilar products, we reduce overall risk. Yet because real estate cannot be easily diversified, how do we reduce risks without being able to diversify? It is not practical to try and purchase dozens of properties in many different cities and in markets with varying growth rates, market rents, and other features. The tax benefits of real estate, which often define the benefit of rental income property investing, may also be limited. For those who cannot write off losses in real estate, this benefit is limited, making ownership of multiple properties impractical.

Diversification is the obvious method for reducing known market risks in the stock market. The same is not true for real estate. Beyond market risk, diversification provides no real protection for the real estate investor; in fact, diversification may increase other forms of risk. The ways to mitigate risk in real estate beyond diversification include the following strategies:

1. *Market risk.* Diversification works only to prevent market risk. This is why it is normally confined to stock market discussions, where market risk is the dominant topic. But in real estate, you also face market risk. Because diversification through the purchase of multiple properties is rarely practical, you need to manage market risks through careful selection of properties. Do not use national trends to judge the market. Look at regional trends and study market price movements over recent

months and years. Check the statistics kept by your local MLS office, and look for trends. The inventory of homes currently on the market, spread between asked and sold prices, and time properties are on the market, are all revealing. The direction of change of those trends is even more valuable.

2. *Rental unit demand risk.* The demand for units, often expressed as occupancy or vacancy rate, tells you about this risk. You cannot diversify rental income property in many different markets because it is too difficult to manage rental income property in distant cities or towns. Thorough research of local markets is a prerequisite, of course. Beyond that, however, you also reduce risks by studying market trends and discovering what types of units remain occupied more than others. For example, lower-cost housing tends to rent out more quickly than high-cost housing, and multiple-unit housing brings better cash flow, as a rule. Some investors prefer buying upscale housing in expensive neighborhoods because, over time, those properties tend to outpace the market. This may be true, but you also need to cover your cash flow in the short term. With that in mind, you may reduce rental unit demand risk by purchasing cheaper duplex and triplex properties. Each unit may draw lower rents than a single-family home, but added together, the total rent may easily exceed the market rent for a single-family home going for the same price.

3. *Tenant conflict risk.* For many people who have bought rental income properties, the worst aspect has been dealing with tenants. Some people know how to take advantage of the rental market, especially in states where landlord/tenant laws favor tenants. The ownership of many properties in different areas increases your tenant conflict risk; the farther away you live from your properties, the more exposure you have to this risk. So diversification is not the answer. The only way to reduce tenant conflict risk is by taking written applications and checking *all* references thoroughly. This includes current and past landlords, bank, employer, and personal references. Do not trust your instincts because some people know exactly how to con others; you need to check everything, including credit reports and criminal or eviction history. (You can find out about these matters for free at your local court clerk's office.) You also reduce this risk by requiring first and last months' rent and a security deposit.

4. *Cash flow risk.* The most severe form of risk you face is the possibility of negative cash flow. Not only does this affect the profitability of rental income property investing; it could also adversely affect your personal budget and even your credit rating. As long as the economic forces

affect all properties within one region, cash flow risk would increase with diversification. The problem of diversifying is that it means acquiring more properties. To mitigate cash flow risk, diversification is *not* the answer. Instead, you need to consider other steps. These include making higher down payments to improve the gap between rental income and payouts; investing in fixer-uppers and then converting to rentals, to further increase the rental/mortgage gap; and taking a position only when market-rate rents are higher than your mortgage payment.

5. *Liquidity risk.* Real estate is considered an illiquid investment. You cannot move money around easily unless you sell, refinance, or acquire more financing. Everyone needs to maintain some level of liquidity, so tying up *more* capital through real estate diversification is contrary to this goal. To maintain liquidity, establish savings accounts, a cash reserve, and other investments where you can easily get your hands on your money if and when you need it. Only then should you be willing to consider putting a large sum of money into a down payment on a rental income property.

6. *Interest rate risk.* If you finance your rental income property with a variable-rate loan, you face the possibility of higher future payments. Variable-rate loans are attractive because initial rates are far lower than those on fixed-rate financing; for some, qualifying for financing may depend on seeking variable-rate financing. However, it is also possible that future interest rates will rise. If that occurs, but market rates for rentals do not, then you face ever-worsening cash flow problems. Clearly, diversification by purchasing many real estate properties is not going to address this risk. To reduce interest rate risk, you need to seek fixed-rate loans, or to be prepared to sell properties within a target range of years. For example, in the fixer-upper market, you may decide to convert improved properties to rentals and then hold for five years before selling. This gives you a comfortable rent/mortgage gap, and also provides a few years of tax benefits. It also minimizes the risk of permanently increasing interest costs, if and when market rates do rise.

Forms of Diversification

Three forms of diversification may be useful to rental income property investors. If you want to be invested in the real estate market, you face the problem of reconciling practical limitations with the desirability of spreading risks.

Product Diversification

Product diversification is the first method for avoiding putting too much of your capital in one place. In some applications, investing in this manner is called asset allocation. Portions of capital are placed into stocks, real estate and the money market (savings, certificates of deposit, and money market funds, for example). However, strictly within the real estate market, you can diversify by product if you make distinctions between different types of real estate.

For example, buying raw land is considered highly speculative, but if you have a good sense of the direction that future growth is likely to take, it can be highly profitable. Raw land produces no cash flow in most situations, so to buy raw land, you need to be able to invest the cash or live with a mortgage payment. At the same time, residential real estate—the favorite among individual investors—has many strong attributes but is subject to changes in the housing and rental unit markets. Some form of diversification is achieved by purchasing multiunit housing: duplex, triplex, or small apartment complexes, for example. You may also consider buying commercial property. A retail or service tenant may be the solution to your desire for diversification; but the commercial market is highly specialized, notably in valuation. You may need expert help in the form of a real estate agent who specializes in commercial properties, as well as an experienced appraiser. Some lenders may also be unwilling to lend money on properties other than residential.

Market Diversification

Market diversification is a second way to manage your real estate portfolio. Within the broad real estate market, individual ownership is only one possible way to invest money. You can also buy units in limited partnerships or master real estate partnerships; or in bond obligation pools. A popular debt-based investment is the *mortgage pool*. Programs like the Federal National Mortgage Association (FNMA), also known as "Fannie Mae," or the Government National Mortgage Association (GNMA) or "Ginnie Mae" are government-sponsored agencies that pool mortgages and sell shares to investors. This enables you to take a diversified debt position in *secured debt* obligations—that is, mortgages of many homeowners. This is also known as the *secondary market* for real estate. The mortgage pool is created when lenders approve loans and then sell those loans to

mortgage pool
a pool of individual mortgages, in which shares or units are purchased by investors in increments; similar to a mutual fund for stocks or bonds, the mortgage pool is an affordable way to diversify a secured debt position in the real estate market.

Valuable Resource

Check the home pages for both of the major mortgage pool agencies, Ginnie Mae and Fannie Mae, at http://www.ginniemae.gov/ and http://www.fanniemae.com/.

secured debt

any debt secured by real property, such as a mortgage. As a borrower, a real estate loan is a secured debt because in the event of default, the lender has a legal claim on the property. As an investor, secured debts such as mortgages are safer than unsecured loans because, if the borrower defaults, the investor (or the mortgage pool management) has a claim on the property.

the organizations. Most people who borrow money to buy real estate have their mortgages transferred in this way, even when the original lender continues to collect monthly mortgage payments. The *mortgage-backed securities* industry is huge. By the end of 2003, the industry held $67.9 billion in investment volume.[1]

The market for mortgage-backed securities is also diverse. For example, it may include limited partnerships, collateralized bond obligations, or any other forms of pooled investments. One of the most popular is the *real estate investment trust (REIT)*. This is a pooled investment in which shares are traded on public exchanges just like stocks. The REIT overcomes the problem of liquidity that is often associated with real estate investing.

The REIT comes in four forms. The safest is the *equity REIT*, in which the program is limited only to acquiring properties without also carrying a mortgage. By collecting investment capital from hundreds (or thousands) of investors, management of the equity REIT reduces cash flow risk by purchasing large real estate projects (such as business and industrial parks, shopping centers, or housing developments). A second type is the *mortgage REIT,* which operates like the larger government-sponsored mortgage pools, but on a smaller scale. For example, a mortgage REIT may be organized to operate in a limited geographic area or to finance a particular type of program. The third type is the *construction and development REIT* which may be the highest-risk form. This REIT is formed specifically to pool investor's money to lend to contractors and developers. Finally, a *hybrid REIT* combines come or all of the features of the other types.

---

[1]Ginnie Mae, <http://www.ginniemae.gov/> (8 February 2005), Government National Mortgage Association.

Use of Money Diversification

Use of money diversification is the third form that may be practical to real estate investors. There are three general ways to invest capital. First is by taking an equity position. The best-known forms of equity investment are real estate ownership and stocks. The second is through debt, the lending of money to someone else in exchange for interest. You are a debt investor when you buy bonds or shares of income mutual funds. You are also a debt investor when you place funds in a savings account or money market fund because your capital is then used to make loans to other people. The final form, one well-known to real estate investors, is leverage. You can use capital for leverage, enabling you to acquire control over a larger amount of capital. When you make a down payment on real estate, you acquire a small portion of equity, but you also leverage a larger amount. For example, a $30,000 down payment on a $100,000 property consists of 30 percent equity and 70 percent leverage. You achieve some diversification when you leverage capital. For example, if you have $60,000 to invest, you may place $30,000 in stocks, and $30,000 in real estate. However, because your real estate down payment leverages an asset of greater value, you have diversified your capital. The alternative—waiting until you can afford to pay cash—is impractical, because you may never have enough available to buy real estate outright.

Why Some Portfolios Are Not Really Diversified

In any discussion of diversification, it is important to question whether a specific strategy truly achieves diversification. If you simply assume that your portfolio is diversified, you may only discover you are wrong when you suffer a large loss. So if your portfolio is not really diversified, you need to take steps to protect your capital.

---

secondary market
a description of the overall market for transfer of mortgage debt. Lenders take applications, approve loans and provide the service of collecting monthly payments, managing escrow impounds, and helping borrowers with questions. However, the actual debt may have been transferred to a mortgage pool, where individual investors may purchase shares of an overall portfolio consisting of hundreds of individual loans.

mortgage-backed securities
debt securities in pools, in which the safety of an investment is represented by a secured mortgage obligation; these securities include mortgage pools as well as partnerships or real estate trusts.

real estate investment trust (REIT)

a pooled investment in real estate, whose shares are traded over public exchanges like stocks; a form of real estate investing that overcomes the common problem of liquidity.

equity REIT

a real estate investment trust formed specifically to acquire equity positions in real estate.

mortgage REIT

a real estate investment trust designed to acquire mortgages and to provide diversified, secured debt positions to investors.

construction and development REIT

a real estate investment trust formed to provide financing to contractors and developers.

For example, if you place *all* of your capital into a single mutual fund, does the natural diversification within that fund protect you? It does not, if the fund specializes in a particular investment goal. An equity fund may be conservative, or it may seek "aggressive long-term growth," meaning its management believes in taking some changes to pursue profits. But if the broad market declines, an aggressive fund loses value across the board, at least in the short term. So how do you diversify?

This question is a constant one in the stock market. In the real estate market, you also need to think about how you achieve real diversification. Clearly, owning several rental income properties in the same city or town is not going to achieve diversification. Owning several properties of different types (residential, commercial, or land, for example) achieves one form of diversification. Owning shares of mortgage pools as well as having equity positions places you on both sides of the interest rate market. For example, if your variable loan's rate increases, your profits in a mortgage pool may increase as well. As owner of leveraged real estate, you are a borrower, but as owner of mortgage pool shares, you are a lender. So in this situation, you have diversified your real estate investments. Risk on one side is offset by higher profits on the other.

This is an oversimplified example because it does not consider the problem of changes in cash flow; but it does make the point. If you limit your investments to only one product or type of product (stocks or mutual funds, or residential real estate, for example) you may not be as diversified as you would like. This is where asset allocation comes into play.

Allocation

It is sometimes difficult to tell the difference between diversification and allocation. In some respects, they mean the same thing—spreading risks. The difference, however, is that diversification usually is applied to a specific type of market risk and within one product (stocks, real estate, money markets, etc.). Allocation refers to a range of different markets and a variety of different market risks.

Allocation is an expansion on diversification, in two respects. First, an allocated portfolio would involve a conscious split of capital among several markets. Second, allocation should be designed to reduce exposure to any one form of market risk. For example, you may decide to allocate your portfolio in a 40/40/20 split—40 percent in stocks, 40 percent in real estate, and 20 percent in savings and money market accounts. This allocation of capital among three markets also diversifies your market risks. Generally, stock market and real estate cycles do not move in the same direction; in fact, market analysts often observe that as money leaves one of these markets, it tends to move into the other. When stocks are perceived as unsafe, investments in real estate increase and vice versa. Leaving some portion of capital in highly liquid savings makes sense as well. This covers a particular form of risk (liquidity) and also further allocates capital outside of stocks and real estate.

> **hybrid REIT**
> a real estate investment trust combining attributes and markets in some combination, including equity and debt positions within the same portfolio.

Expanded allocation may call for placing some portion of investment capital in other areas, such as precious metals or collectibles, for example. Some investors also like to put aside a portion of their capital for pure speculation, investing that money in options or commodities. The specific decisions you make regarding allocation depend on (1) your experience and knowledge as an investor; (2) the amount of capital available to you; (3) your income and ability to accept cash flow risks; and (4) your personal risk tolerance level. Not every investor has the same tolerance levels and, as the other attributes change, your risk tolerance will change as well. For example, if you have lost a large amount of capital in the stock market, you might decide to assign a far lower allocation to stocks, and even limit your investment to conservative mutual fund shares. If you have had negative experiences with tenants, you might decide to limit your real estate activity to flipping of fixer-upper properties over the short term, combined with pooled mortgage investing. The point is that experience, income and available capital all affect your personal risk tolerance.

Risk tolerance is also going to be affected by major changes in your life: Marriage, birth of a child, purchasing a first home, divorce, health problems, the death of a loved one, losing a job, changing careers, and retirement are among the major changes you can experience. All of these events are likely change your risk tolerance. For example, when a child is born, you might decide you need to increase your life insurance coverage, buy a home, or improve your job skills. Some events, especially those beyond our control, can have a disastrous effect on risk tolerance. A family member's death, personal bankruptcy, divorce, long-term disability or health problems have unplanned negative impact. Unexpected changes on the positive side like winning a lottery or inheriting millions of dollars also turn your financial planning upside down and change the whole picture.

The specific strategies you select today to diversify your money in order to spread risks, or to allocate assets to change the types of risks you face, are temporary. Each time you go through a change in fortunes, whether positive, negative or just part of life, your risk tolerance will be changed immediately. So today's decisions concerning diversification and allocation only work as long as your current person, family and earnings status remains unchanged, too.

Review and Change

The very fact that things change requires that you go through a periodic review of your portfolio. The periodic review enables you to change your investing posture based on evolving attitudes. Once a life-altering event has occurred, it may be too late to take defensive action in your portfolio. Therefore, a review should occur at least once a year and more often if your investment portfolio is complex or if many changes are taking place in your life. For example, your family could be expecting a child. You could inherit money. You could be starting a new business. You could be closing on your first home. There is the potential for a lot to be going on. You need to review your portfolio more frequently than when things are quieter.

The periodic review may be a sole effort or one that spouses go through together. You may decide to make your own decisions or listen to a trusted adviser—a stockbroker or financial planner, for example. Be sure that any changes you make are based on your personal risk profile and circumstances. A common mistake is to make important investment decisions because someone makes a recommendation that is *not* based on your profile or needs. That is a mistake.

Changes you make in your portfolio or allocation between investment markets are very important decisions. If you currently have a savings account and also own shares of stock and mutual fund shares, what happens if you decide to buy a fixer-upper or a rental property? For example, say you currently have $80,000 invested: $45,000 is in stocks and $35,000 is in saving. You are thinking about buying a rental income property, using $30,000 as a down payment. That would change your current allocation among stocks, real estate, and savings from 56/0/44 to an allocation of 56/38/6. This shifts from highly liquid 44 percent to a 38 percent illiquid and only 6 percent liquid—a significant change. This shift in allocation may be justified considering current market values and growth potential, the desirability of tax benefits, and your willingness to accept cash flow risks. All of these points should be considered as part of the decision to shift allocation. This example shows that the change is an important one. Not only is the allocation shifted, the risk attributes will change as well.

Decisions to change allocation should be made with those changes in mind, and not just because a particular investment choice is appealing. This point—the importance of long-term planning and control—is the topic for the next chapter.

Chapter

A Long-Term
Investment View

Every type of investment has its own unique mix of attributes, both positive and negative. Real estate investors enjoy tremendous tax benefits not available to others; average real estate values have consistently risen over many years; and rental income is used to pay the mortgage so that investors are able to leverage their capital. On the downside, real estate investors have to be concerned about the prospect of negative cash flow, a slow market, unpleasant tenants, and the basic illiquidity of real estate itself.

Any investment you choose will contain a similar balance between positive and negative attributes. This is unavoidable. It makes perfect sense to invest in rental income property as long as you know these attributes in advance and accept them. When you consider the same attributes for stocks or savings accounts, you soon realize that, in fact, allocating capital among several different areas makes sense.

Cash Flow versus Profits

Avoid the common mistakes made by rental income investors; be aware of the pitfalls and avoid them. If you select the fixer-upper market as your investment of choice, you need to plan ahead, gathering information on the cost of repairs, the time involved, and the feasibility of performing a specific series of improvements. Some cosmetic repairs have great potential for returning a fast profit on your efforts, while others are going to be a cash drain. Before proceeding, you need to determine which types of repairs fit into each classification.

Investor Mistake 1: Neglecting to identify which repairs return profits in a fixer-upper investment.

Carefully chosen fixer-upper properties can be turned around quickly and sold at a profit. The ideal situation is one in which you place the newly acquired property on the market soon after purchase, and execute cosmetic repairs as quickly as possible. The profit equation for fixer-upper properties is to minimize interest expense. This requires that you identify repairs you can complete within a fast schedule. A property with expensive repairs, or one you need to hold longer than you thought, only drains your profits.

Investor Mistake 2: Assuming you can get a quick sale for improved fixer-upper properties and ignoring the current market trend.

If you make a mistake in the selection of a fixer-upper, you might need to convert it to a rental income property to stop the outlay of cash. By holding a property for a few years, you could wait out the market and eventually get your investment back out. While this might be the most sensible alternative, it is far from desirable. If you have picked fixer-uppers as your preferred strategy, ending up with rentals ties up capital and requires you to deal with tenants. Therefore, the decision comes down to how much drain on cash flow you can afford; how you feel about tenants; and how long you have to keep a property before you can sell it at a profit.

Investor Mistake 3: Over-spending on a fixer-upper and being forced to convert it to a long-term rental that cannot be sold profitably.

Another alternative is to move into the fixer-upper property. This can be done by design, or it can be a choice that you make later when you discover that you have overspent on a property. You may even decide to move into the property while you continue to work on repairing and improving it. As a general rule, moving a family into such a property can be highly stressful and, for many people, simply does not work. A single person or a young couple without children can adjust to this arrangement; and in that case, your spouse should be enthusiastic about working with you on the fixer-upper venture.

Investor Mistake 4: Moving the family into a fixer-upper when a spouse is not supportive, does not have a choice, or does not want to live in a property in disrepair.

The cash flow issue is equally important when you own rental income property for the long term. Before buying any property, go through the numbers. How much rent can you charge? How much will your mortgage payments be each month? How much are your other expenses? Do the numbers work out? If you discover that you have negative cash flow even when your property is rented every month, it makes no sense to purchase that property.

Investor Mistake 5: Investing in rental income property without checking the numbers and ending up with negative cash flow that would have been easily identified in advance.

An expensive mistake is to assume that market value is going to outpace negative cash flow. It will not necessarily happen and, equally important, you may not be able to afford the net outlay of cash every month. What happens if you have a three-month vacancy? Can you afford to make the mortgage payment without also getting the rent each month?

Investor Mistake 6: Accepting marginal or negative cash flow while depending on growth in market value to outpace the cash outlay.

These questions make the point that cash flow is a more serious and important matter than long-term profits. If your rental income investment is going to work, you have to be able to afford it, even given the contingency of vacancies or unexpected repairs.

Investor Mistake 7: Investing in rental income property with marginal cash flow when unexpected repairs or vacancies would make the venture unfeasible.

Identifying the Profit Margin

The key to investment profits is identifying the *profit margin*, the difference between income and costs. If you buy shares of stock, you hope to sell at a higher price than the purchase price. When you calculate the transaction costs, the net difference between the dollar amounts paid and received is the margin. When you buy rental income property, the same calculation is involved but it is more complex.

When you buy a fixer-upper, your basis includes the purchase price plus closing costs; interest on the

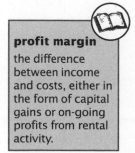

profit margin
the difference between income and costs, either in the form of capital gains or on-going profits from rental activity.

mortgage loan for the period you own the property; and the cost of repairs and improvements. The profit margin is the difference between basis and costs on one side, and net sales price on the other. The net sales price is reduced by the closing costs upon sale.

When you keep properties as rentals, the profit margin has two different definitions. For as long as you own the property, the year-to-year profit is the difference between rental income and rental expenses. Those expenses include interest, property taxes, insurance, utilities, and other cash paid out. However, you also include the noncash expense for depreciation as part of the profit margin. The difference between profits and cash flow is further complicated. If you spend money on capital improvements, it reduces cash flow but does not reduce profits; and you have to calculate tax benefits as an increase to cash flow.

The second version of profit margin is the capital gain upon sale of a rental income property. This is a complex calculation, for several reasons:

1. *The after-tax basis is not easy to calculate.* What is the true after-tax profit margin on a rental income investment? Do you reduce profits by the capital gain and tax on depreciation recapture? (Remember, also, that whereas maximum tax on long-term capital gains is limited to 15 percent, recapture taxes go as high as 25 percent.) A consistent method for figuring out your profit margin is difficult to find, because the transactions are complex and often involve multiple tax years.

2. *The holding period affects the annualized yield.* If you own a fixer-upper for three months and earn a profit of $6,000, how do you compare that to a rental income property you hold for six years and make a $12,000 profit? The fixer-upper annualized out to a profit equal to $24,000 (three-month holding period), but the $12,000 profit annualizes out to only $2,000 per year, on average. When you calculate annualized yield, the whole picture changes. Annualizing may be less reliable as a comparative tool for real estate than for stocks, but the question cannot be ignored. Clearly, the more quickly you turn investments over, the higher the annualized yield.

3. *Annual tax benefits affect the overall profitability.* In calculating profit margin on rental income properties, how do you allow for the year-to-year tax benefits? We have seen that these benefits can create a situation of positive cash flow, but does that also affect overall profitability upon sale? You want to keep your calculations simple; but if you have to put a lot of cash into maintaining one property, while another is a cash cow, the overall profit margin on each will also be dissimilar.

4. *Profitability should be based on actual cash invested.* To accurately calculate your profit margin, your calculation should be based on cash-in,

cash-out. So you begin with your down payment, not changes in over-all property value. For example, if you buy a property for $100,000 and put $30,000 down, and later sell it for $130,000, have you made 30 percent ($30,000 increase in property value) or have you doubled your money ($30,000 profit on a $30,000 down payment)? The most accurate and consistent method is to always base your calculations on net cash invested and taken out.

This suggestion simplifies all of the calculations and makes comparisons the same between properties. To figure out the true profit margin on rental income property, you should include:

- The net cash received or paid throughout the year
- The cash benefit from reduced taxes (for example, if a reported tax loss reduces your tax liabilities by $2,000—that is extra cash and it should be counted)
- Cash invested in the basis of property (down payment, closing costs, and capital improvements)
- Net cash received upon sale (sales price minus closing costs)
- Reduction of overall capital gain for the difference that profit makes in your tax liability (For example, if your capital gain of $30,000 creates an additional tax liability of $10,000, it reduces your cash to a net profit margin from capital gain of $20,000.)
- Overall total calculated on an average annual basis (For example, if you originally invested $30,000 and ended up receiving $50,000 and your holding period was four years, your profit margin was $20,000, and your annualized cash profits were $5,000.)

The Importance of Turnover

Annualizing your profit margin makes the point that turnover affects the calculation. The more quickly you produce the dollar amount of profits, the higher the *yield*. Profit margin is usually reported as the dollar amount of profits, whereas yield is the percentage it represents of your base investment. For example, if you invest $30,000 and end up receiving $50,000 the profit margin of $20,000 represents an overall yield of 67% ($20,000 ÷ $30,000). But if you held the property for four years, the annualized yield is 16.75% (67% ÷ 4).

yield
the profit from investments, expressed as a yield. Annualized yield is expressed as the overall yield, adjusted as though the investment were held for exactly one year.

turnover
the number of times capital is reused to produce profits. The more frequently capital is turned over, the greater overall yield will be, assuming the desired profit margin is earned.

If you are able to produce quick profits in fixer-uppers, your annualized yield will be higher. This becomes important in fixer-upper activity. The more frequently you reuse the same investment capital, the higher your profit margin *and* the higher your annualized yield. Because interest expense is significant when you are not offsetting mortgage payments with rental income, quick *turnover* is an important factor in fixer-upper investing. In fact, if you do not achieve the desired turnover rate for capital, your profits will not justify the activity.

A study of the numbers makes this point. Assume you target a fixer-upper property on the assumption that you can make a profit margin of $3,000 on a $30,000 investment. That investment consists of a $20,000 down payment plus a budget of $10,000 for improvements and ongoing interests payments on the mortgage. Obviously, the longer you keep the property, the more interest you pay and the less profit you earn. If you are forced to keep the property for too long, the marginal profits will be quickly absorbed by interest. Therefore, it is essential to equate the target profit margin with the holding period; in other words, you need to know in advance how rapidly you will need to turn over the investment. If you can sell in three months, your $3,000 profit margin is a 10 percent yield; annualized, that is a 40 percent yield. However, if you end up holding the property for six months and your profit margin erodes down to only $1,500, it is a 5 percent yield, or an annualized 10 percent yield. A holding period of an additional three months cuts the annualized yield from 40 percent down to 10 percent.

In the fixer-upper market, turnover defines the difference between an acceptable yield and a less than acceptable yield. When the target profit margin is small, you depend on the fast turnover to justify your time, effort, and risk. If the market slows down and your property does not sell as quickly as you assume it will, that yield will evaporate quickly. So turnover is at the core of fixer-upper profitability.

Turnover is less of an immediate issue when you plan to hold properties as long-term rentals. In that case, your concern is more for month-to-month cash flow and, if applicable, for annual tax benefits. Even if you hold properties for only a few years, the game plan involves having rental income cover expenses and payments; and depending on growth in market value to make the investment profitable over time. This is the most likely scenario. In fact, using leverage, it is possible to achieve a form of turnover to increase your investment base and long-term profitability. When equity accumulates in your rental properties, it may be possible to use that equity through refinancing to free up money to purchase additional rental income properties.

The concept of leveraging indefinitely may be exciting, but it is not practical. Positive cash flow often depends on annual tax benefits, and those are limited to $25,000 per year at most. So if you own four properties and come up to the $25,000 maximum, you would not increase the tax benefits by buying four more properties. Additionally, lenders are not going to be willing to provide financing indefinitely to enable you to acquire a large number of rental properties. At some point, the cash flow numbers cease to work and you can no longer qualify for a new loan. This is especially true when you are continually taking equity out of existing properties. This increases your debt service and reduces your cash flow margins, so that lenders will put the brakes on additional borrowing once your borrowing ratios no longer work.

Some advertised programs promise no money down plans that will create vast fortunes in real estate. In practice, that concept is very difficult, and most people will not be able to become millionaires overnight. The truth is, the only people who get rich on those plans are the groups selling seminar packages or courses that allegedly tell you how to succeed in real estate.

Fixer-Uppers and Your Financial Plan

The very idea of beginning a real estate investment plan is a serious one. It needs to be coordinated as part of your overall long-term financial plan. It has often been said that buying a home is the largest purchase most people ever make. By the same argument, buying fixer-upper property is the largest investment that most people ever make.

The cash flow challenges are only the beginning of the risk analysis that you will need to go through to ensure that you understand exactly what you expect to happen; how much profit you are likely to gain; and what specific risks you face along the way. As a fixer-upper expert, you will need to master the budgeting requirements for numerous cosmetic and other repairs, and also to be able to estimate the time required to complete those repairs. Finally, you need to analyze potential profit margins and assess those against the probable time requirement to bring a run-down property up to standards.

You are not limited in the creative methods you may use to achieve your profit margin. For example, perhaps you or your spouse should take the exam to become a real estate agent. In this manner, you can cut your commission upon sale in half. Generally, an agent receives one-half of the commission and the broker gets the other half. (In cases where an agent, other than the listing agent, brings a buyer to the table, the commission could be split four ways because an outside agent and broker would be involved.) The potential for earning a real estate commission by having the license is worth considering. You may also try to sell properties on your own. While the potential market exposure may not be as

FSBO

real estate jargon meaning For Sale By Owner, that is, an individual who sells property without using the services of a real estate agent.

broad, you may be able to make a far more attractive margin on your property by acting as an *FSBO* (For Sale By Owner). For example, if the commission is 6 percent on a $150,000 property, the commission will be $9,000. By selling on your own (assuming you get a full-price offer) you increase your profits by $9,000, or you gain more flexibility in how much of an offer you could accept below your asked price.

If you decide to work without an agent, remember these points:

1. *The agent's job is limited to finding buyers and working with sellers.* For the most part, the agent is nothing more than a person who brings buyers and sellers together. The suggestion that the agent offers financial advice is simply wrong.

2. *An escrow agent or banker can help you organize your paperwork.* Many people shy away from FSBO sales because they are nervous about the paperwork. Your initial offer is a standard form and can be completed easily and without guidance from an agent. Your local escrow officer, banker or real estate attorney can provide you with a copy of the standard real estate agreement form.

3. *You can also negotiate your real estate commission.* If you try selling on your own and it does not work out, you can always enter into a listing agreement later. Remember, though, that you do *not* have to pay the full commission. Negotiate the percentage down below the standard 6 or 7 percent that agents usually charge. And under no circumstances should you pay the full rate on amounts over the first $100,000. It is common to negotiate one commission on the first $100,000 and half that level for anything above.

These are important planning points. The money you save on reduced real estate commissions could represent a significant part of your profits. However, even beyond this, your overall financial plan is going to be affected by your decision to invest money in fixer-upper properties. You need to discuss the decision with your spouse *and* with a financial planner. Be aware that planners may earn their income by either a commission or a consultation fee; they are not supposed to earn both. If you consult with a planner working on a commission basis, they may discourage you from proceeding with a fixer-upper and try to steer you into products on which they will be paid. This would not serve you well, because the planner would not be advising you on the idea *you* have. You are better off working with a planner who works for an hourly or set fee, because that person is more likely to give you objective advice; remind you of the cash flow risks and other risks; and assist with a comparison between your fixer-upper ideas and other choices—the kind of help you will need to make your own decision.

Long-Term Rentals and Your Financial Plan

The cash flow, market, and other risks of investing in rental income properties, is much different than the attributes for fixer-uppers. You would expect to begin earning cash flow from the moment your purchases closes. As soon as you find a tenant and enter into an agreement, your cash flow begins. In the ideal situation, you can achieve positive monthly cash flow *and* a net tax loss due to the benefits of writing off depreciation.

You can invest in as many as four of five properties and still create net losses within the limitation of the $25,000 annual maximum. This does not necessarily mean that you should have that many properties. But it serves as a likely maximum. Some people have been able to build a portfolio of rental properties by moving from one to another and converting the previous primary residence to a rental. This is advantageous in the type of financing you will be able to acquire, and also in the level of down payment.

As a general rule, if you tell a lender that you are trying to buy a property as your primary residence, you do have to move into that property. However, there is no rule stating that you must remain there and continue to use it as your primary residence. When you seek a loan for your own home, the lender may require only 10 percent down, or in some cases nothing down. This depends on the loan terms, your credit, and the relationship between the mortgage payment and your monthly income. You are also likely to get an attractive interest rate; lenders view primary residences as lower risks than investment properties.

In comparison, investment properties require higher down payments—often 30 percent—and may also be based on higher interest rate levels. Lenders may also use tighter restrictions, so you may not qualify for an investment property while you could qualify for financing of a primary residence. For that reason, as long as you move into the property and use it as a primary residence at the outset, you are free to seek a *new* primary residence and additional financing once the deal closes. You cannot mislead the lender by telling them you will use the property as your primary residence if, in fact, you do not intend to do so. However, you can wait a few months and decide to convert the property and move to yet another newly acquired property.

As long as you are honest with your lenders, it is possible to acquire financing for a series of properties in this manner. To ensure that you meet the rules, ask the lender how long you are required to live in the property to consider it your primary residence and to qualify for financing. There is not really an answer to this. The only rule requires that at the time you seek financing, you must be planning to move into the property. If you are mobile enough to be able to do that, there is no specific restriction on changing your mind later.

The point to remember is that, as part of your initial financial planning, you want to get the most attractive terms possible. As long as you are up front with your lender about your strategies, you are allowed to move as often as you wish. As long as your cash flow analysis works out, you are not limited as to the number of properties you can own, remembering the annual cap on deductible net losses.

Checklist: The Key Ingredients

The 10 key ingredients to remember when thinking about buying fixer-upper or rental income properties are:

1. Cash flow is more urgent than long-term profits.

2. Tax benefits for real estate investors are significant, and often make the difference between positive or negative cash flow.

3. The maximum annual deductible loss from real estate is $25,000. This maximum may be reduced when your modified adjusted gross income is more than $100,000.

4. Investing in rental income properties complicates your tax reporting requirements.

5. The key risk elements in fixer-uppers are time and cost—the more time and the higher your costs, the lower your profits.

6. The key risk elements in long-term rental income investing are cash flow, potential tenant problems, and the level of demand for rental units.

7. Diversification is a useful method for reducing market risks; but for real estate, diversification could actually increase overall risks. To manage a portfolio of real estate, you need to look beyond the concept of buying multiple properties to spread market risk.

8. Asset allocation is one way to reduce risks, and may consist of buying dissimilar kinds of real estate; combining equity, debt and leverage positions; and planning your overall portfolio to consciously determine portions to invest in real estate and elsewhere.

9. Your profit margin and annualized yield are ultimately determined in the case of fixer-uppers, by turnover.

10. Your long-term yield in rental income investing has to consider annual tax benefits, taxes on capital gains, net profit margin between purchase and sale, and annual cash flow. The calculation should be based on the net cash in or out, and calculated on an annualized basis.

Your real estate venture can be highly positive and rewarding, assuming that you perform your analysis in advance, and that you are willing to assume the inevitable risks involved. While risk is present in all forms of investing, the risks of real estate are not the same as those for other markets, such as the stock market. You need to perform a different kind of fundamental analysis to make informed decisions. However, once you understand the relationship between risk and income potential, rental income investments provide fewer problems and more benefits than most of the alternatives.

Glossary

accelerated depreciation a method of calculating depreciation in which a larger amount can be deducted in the early years of useful life and less in later years. This system is allowed for autos and trucks, computers, and office equipment, but is not allowed for improvements to real estate, which have to be depreciated under the straight-line method.

active participation status of investors in rental income properties when they make decisions concerning tenant selection, rent levels, repairs, and buying or selling; active participation is a requisite for deducting annual net losses from rental income activity.

adjusted gross income (AGI) for tax purposes, your total income after claiming adjustments for IRA, student loan interest, tuition, moving expenses, self-employment tax, alimony paid, and certain other items; and before calculating itemized or standard deduction or tax credits.

adjusted purchase price the original price at which property is purchased, plus all costs paid by the buyer to acquire the property. These costs include inspection fee, escrow, title insurance, legal fees paid, recording and documentation fees, and other expenses required to be paid by the buyer.

adjusted sales price the price at which property is sold, minus all costs of sale. Costs include real estate commissions paid as well as all other seller expenses: recording fees, reconveyance, partial payments of utilities, interest and taxes; and expenses paid for improvements in anticipation of the sale.

allocated expenses those expenses, not directly attributable to any specific property, that are assigned to two or more properties (including professional fees, office supplies, and auto expenses, for example). The most consistent method for allocating expenses is on the basis of rents collected.

amortization (mortgage loan) the gradual reduction of a balance over time, based on the interest rate and time involved. In the case of the typical mortgage loan, interest is calculated each month as 1/12th of the annual rate, applied against the current loan balance.

amortization (rental expense) an annual expense for items not deductible in one year, such as points charged by a lender, which must be amortized over the full loan period.

annualized yield the rate of return earned on an investment, calculated as if that investment were held for exactly one year. To calculate, divide the dollar amount of return by the dollar amount invested; divide the percentage by the number of months the investment was owned; and then multiply the result by 12 (months).

asset allocation   an expansion of investment diversification, in which percentages of total capital are invested in dissimilar types of investments, such as stocks, real estate, or cash deposits.

balloon payment   a specific date in the future on which the entire balance of a loan is due and payable. In an interest-only loan, borrowers are required to pay interest each month, on the understanding that a balloon payment is to be made to repay the principal balance.

book value   the net value recorded after depreciation has been calculated. Once an asset has been fully depreciation, book value is zero, even if the asset continues to have market value.

bridge loan   a form of financing granted during construction or, for fixer-upper properties, for a limited number of months during which repairs are completed. Interest accumulates during the bridge period, but no payments are required until the bridge period has expired.

capital improvements   all changes made to land including the building itself and, following purchase, costs such as additions, a new roof, and other costs that are above and beyond the normal expenses of the property, such as repairs and maintenance.

carry   taking a loan on property; when a seller agrees to carry the loan, it means the seller transfers title to the buyer and then takes on the role of lender.

cash buyer   anyone who plans to pay cash for property, and who will not need to go through financing qualification. Real estate agents often persuade sellers to list with them because they claim to have a cash buyer, meaning the deal could close quickly. In practice, few cash buyers exist.

cash flow   the amount of cash moving in and out within an investment program. Cash flow has to be manageable in order to justify the investment, based on income, expenses, nondeductible payments, and tax benefits.

competition   a basic theory of economics in real estate, that the greater the number of competing properties for sale, the greater the tendency for prices to be dilutes; and when competition is low, prices may be driven upward due to greater demand.

conformity   a principle in real estate observing that housing values of similar properties tend to move in the same direction and at the same rate; and that homes with dissimilar features and attributes do not appreciate in value in the same way.

construction and development REIT   a real estate investment trust formed to provide financing to contractors and developers.

Consumer Price Index (CPI)   the best-known measurement of inflation, an index developed to measure changes in prices from one year to the next, in many categories. The CPI indicates the health of the economy, especially in major markets, including housing prices.

contingency   a clause in a real estate offer providing performance in the event that certain events occur or do not occur. Payment for inspections is a common example, and contingency clauses can further specify responsibility to pay for repairs, contingencies related to obtaining financing, selling other property, or other forms of performance by the buyer or by the seller, including deadlines for completion.

debt service   payments to a lender required each month, consisting of principal and interest and, if applicable, impounds for property taxes and insurance.

depreciation   a deduction for the value of capital assets, such as improvements to real estate, allowable over a period of years rather than in the year of purchase.

discount   the difference between a fixer-upper's asked price and average market value of similar homes that do not need repairs or improvements.

distressed properties   real estate available at a discount due to an owner's financial problems or poor condition, which may be quickly flipped and sold at a profit.

diversification   a method for reducing risk by placing capital in several different products; the purpose is to avoid a large loss if and when economic conditions cause price declines in a particular market sector.

effective tax rate   the rate of taxes you pay, combining federal and state liabilities, based on income levels. The effective rate is the rate you will pay based on your current taxable income. Any additional income will be subject to tax at the effective rate and any reductions in taxable income will reduce tax liabilities by the same rate.

elections   decisions to use depreciation methods other than the prescribed general methods. Elections are usually irrevocable and apply to all assets in a specific recovery period.

equity REIT   a real estate investment trust formed specifically to acquire equity positions in real estate.

fair market value   the realistic and competitive price for real estate on today's market, based on average sales for similar properties in recent weeks or months.

fast sale price   the price for real estate set to get a fast sale; a discount from fair market value established to close as quickly as possible.

financing demand   the demand for money that can be used to lend in real estate transactions. As lenders' interest rates rise and fall, their policies and offers vary based on the money supply. When money is plentiful, rates are low and closing terms will be offered at attractive rates; when money is scarce, interest rates are higher, and it will cost more to move through the borrowing process.

firm price   the price set by a seller who is not willing to accept a discount; a price based on fair market value, usually indicating that the seller is not in a hurry to find a buyer or to negotiate the sales price.

fixer-upper   a property priced below current market prices because work needs to be performed, which offers the potential for fast profits as long as repairs can be performed without great expense and in a short period of time.

flipping   a strategy for quick turnaround of real estate; the buy-fix-sell process is intended to produce a net profit as quickly as possible.

FSBO   real estate jargon meaning For Sale by Owner, an individual who sells property without using the services of a real estate agent.

fundamental analysis   the evaluation of investments based on financial information. In the stock market, fundamentals are found primarily in the study of corporate financial statements; in real estate, fundamentals include an evaluation of market supply and demand, prices and discounts available, rental demand levels, and potential for long-term price appreciation.

gap financing a form of financing designed for developers, builders, and investors in fixer-upper properties. A limited time period in which no payments are required, enables fixer-upper investors to complete repairs without concern for cash flow, with the loan and interest payable at the end of the period.

half-year convention the method for calculating first-year depreciation for assets used in conjunction with real estate other than the property itself; this includes most vehicles, office equipment, landscaping equipment and appliances.

highest and best use a reference to property valuation, the observation that value is likely to be maximized when the property is used in the most suitable manner; and that values will be depressed when it is not utilized to its maximum potential.

home equity line of credit financing based on the equity in your home. A lender grants the borrower a line of credit up to a specific level determined by the level of equity, and that line is used by writing a check, and repaid at monthly payment minimums or upon the sale of a fixer-upper, in a lump sum. The line can be used repeatedly.

hybrid REIT a real estate investment trust combining attributes and markets in some combination, including equity and debt positions within the same portfolio.

illiquidity a condition of an investment in which cash cannot be moved in and out easily. Real estate investments are illiquid because cash can be removed only through refinancing debt or selling.

impounds amounts included in a monthly mortgage payment beyond principal and interest, required under the terms of some mortgage contracts. Typical impounds are collected monthly for property taxes and insurance. The lender then makes periodic payments for those obligations.

interest-only loan a loan granted with requirements for interest payments each month but no requirement to repay principal; such loans have a balloon payment clause at some identified point in the future.

inventory the homes currently on the market, expressed both in number of properties and months' of availability. For example, today there are 206 properties for sale. Typically, 38 homes are sold per month. There is a 5.4 month inventory available (206 ÷ 38).

investment risk any form of risk you accept as part of how your investments are structured. In the case of rental income investments, the need for leverage adds risk, because you depend on rental income to be able to afford monthly mortgage payments.

leverage the use of capital to control or to purchase assets worth far more; rental income is applied to paying the cost of leveraged capital, specifically its debt service.

like-kind exchange (1031 exchange) in tax law, the replacement of one property with another of the same general classification. A like-kind exchange, properly executed, creates a deferral of tax liabilities until the replacement property is sold.

lipstick repairs   a level of fixer-upper requiring strictly cosmetic types of work and no structural, expensive, or system-related work.

liquidity   a market condition referring to the ease of buying and selling, or the availability of cash. A highly liquid market (like the stock market) allows investors to move cash in and out of positions cheaply and quickly. Illiquid markets (like directly owned real estate) require complex and expensive closings to buy and sell investments; or refinancing or additional mortgages to remove cash.

margin of profit   the difference between your investment and sale prices. Investment basis consists of original price plus closing costs; repair and improvement expenses; and interest expense on the mortgage. Closing price is the net amount received after closing costs. Margin of profit is expressed as a percentage of the investment basis.

market demand   the demand for property, reflected in price trends of housing; when demand rises, property prices rise as well, especially if housing is scarce. When an excess of housing is available, the demand levels off and prices flatten or decline.

market risk   the primary risk to investing money, that value will fall either temporarily or permanently. Market risk exists in all forms of investing but it varies by degree. The most effective way to offset market risk is through research and analysis before purchase.

material participation   a level of involvement required to qualify for deduction of net losses from rental income activity. Individuals must own at least 10 percent of a property to qualify for deduction of annual net losses.

mid-month convention   the method for calculating first-year depreciation for residential real estate. It is based on the month that the real estate purchase occurs.

Multiple Listing Service (MLS)   a subscription service available to real estate agents reporting all homes currently on the market. The MLS also includes valuable statistics about the current state of supply and demand in the market.

modified AGI   adjusted gross income excluding IRA contributions, student loan interest, taxable Social Security benefits, interest on student loans, self-employment tax, and tuition.

Modified Accelerated Cost Recovery System, (MACRS)   the set of rules and restrictions concerning depreciation and how it has to be reported.

month-to-month   a type of rental agreement in which landlord and tenant continue the rental from one month to the next. In comparison, a lease binds both sides for the entire lease period.

mortgage pool   a pool of individual mortgages, in which shares or units are purchased by investors in increments; similar to a mutual fund for stocks or bonds, the mortgage pool is an affordable way to diversify a secured debt position in the real estate market.

mortgage REIT   a real estate investment trust designed to acquire mortgages and to provide diversified, secured debt positions to investors.

mortgage-backed securities   debt securities in pools, in which the safety of an invest-ment is represented by a secured mortgage obligation; these securities include mortgage pools as well as partnerships or real estate trusts.

negative cash flow   a situation in which rental income property investors have to pay more money out than they receive from rents.

neighborhood in transition   an area in which the quality of housing, maintenance levels, appearance, and social trends such as crime levels are changing. In a positive tran-sition, older homes are improved, renovated and updated in preparation for turnover to a new generation of owners. In a negative transition, lowered demand is characterized by empty and boarded-up homes, empty lots, and increased crime levels.

net breakeven point   the rate of return you need when considering the effects of in-flation and income taxes. To be completely accurate, the effective tax rate should in-clude both federal and state tax rates.

net market value the true fair market value of property, represented by the difference between current market value less the cost of repairs.

occupancy rate   the level of occupancy, expressed as a percentage. For example, a rental property was occupied 10.5 months last year. Occupancy rate was 87.5% (10.5 ÷ 12). On a statistical level, all rentals indicate the local trend. For example, in your area, a total of 1,462 units exist and currently, 1,391 are occupied. The occupancy rate is 95.1% (1,391 ÷ 1,462). This statistic is often expressed as "vacancy rate," which is the opposite, or the percentage of available rental space not occupied.

passive activity   any investment in which the individual is not directly involved in the day-to-day management of properties. Passive losses cannot be deducted, but have to be applied against offsetting passive gains or carried forward to future tax years.

PITI   a term describing a monthly mortgage payment that includes all four elements: principal, interest, taxes and insurance.

points   a cost of borrowing charged by lenders, equal to one percent of the amount to be borrowed. Also called "loan origination fees," points reflect the current availability of money to loan. When the money supply is plentiful, lenders tend to reduce fees, and when money is scarce, points and other fees tend to rise.

positive cash flow   a desirable position in which more cash is being received in rental income, than is being paid out in expenses and debt service. True cash flow should be calculated on an after-tax basis to allow for tax liabilities or benefits.

premium   a price higher than face value; in the case of real estate, if a fixer-upper's asked price is higher than the fair discounted market value, then that price is a premium above net market value.

primary residence   for tax purposes, the property you designate as your home; you can only have one primary residence at any given time. Gain on the sale of a qualified primary resident is tax-free up to $500,000 in net profits.

principle of progression   a theory of real estate valuation, stating that the value of lower priced properties is likely to increase due to proximity to higher-priced or higher-quality properties.

principle of regression   the theory of real estate valuation stating that higher-priced property values may be held back or even reduced due to their proximity to lower-priced properties.

profit margin   the difference between income and costs, either in the form of capital gains or on-going profits from rental activity.

property management company   an independent company specializing in managing rental income properties for investors. They advertise properties, screen tenants, collect rents, manage the property bank account, keep records, and handle normal maintenance (yard work, periodic repairs) as well as unusual problems (tenant or neighbor complaints, for example). The level of control by the company, versus involvement by the investor, may determine whether the individual meets the active participation test for tax purposes.

rate cap   in a variable rate mortgage, contractual terms limiting how much interest rate increases are allowed. Two forms of cap are normally involved: an annual limitation expressed in the number of interest points, and a lifetime cap defining the maximum rate a lender is allowed to charge.

ready market   a market in which a high level of activity and interest are found; where buyers and sellers and quickly and easily execute trades; where margins may be thin; and in which changes in price levels may be rapid.

real estate cycle   the supply and demand cycle for real estate. When the cycle is an a low point, prices are depressed or flat, and houses take longer to sell; as the market demand begins to rise, more building activity occurs and prices rise.

real estate fundamental indicators   the market facts that define whether it is prudent to invest in real estate. These indicators include supply and demand and its effect on current prices; levels of demand for rental real estate units; the cost of borrowing money to finance a purchase; and a comparison between market rates you expect to receive and debt service and other payments you will be required to make.

real estate investment trust (REIT)   a pooled investment in real estate, whose shares are traded over public exchanges like stocks; a form of real estate investing that overcomes the common problem of liquidity.

recapture   a rule in the tax code requiring that the sum of all depreciation deducted while the property is owned, is to be added to the profit (or deducted from the loss) at the time the property is sold.

recovery period   the class of assets, defining the number of years in the useful life, which mandates the calculation of depreciation and the method (accelerated or straight-line) that can be used.

rental demand   the current level of demand, or the number of tenants seeking rentals versus the number of rental units available. Rental demand levels determine market rates as well as vacancy levels and duration.

risk management   the process investors use to evaluate, control, and reduce various forms of investment risk; the methods by which exposure to loss is controlled while potential for profits are kept in place.

risk tolerance   the level of risk an individual is willing and able to take with capital, based on personal income, family situation, and investing experience.

secondary market   a description of the overall market for transfer of mortgage debt. Lenders take applications, approve loans and provide the service of collecting monthly payments, managing escrow impounds, and helping borrowers with questions. However, the actual debt may have been transferred to a mortgage pool, where individual investors may purchase shares of an overall portfolio consisting of hundreds of individual loans.

secured debt   any debt secured by real property, such as a mortgage. As a borrower, a real estate loan is a secured debt because in the event of default, the lender has a legal claim on the property. As an investor, secured debts such as mortgages are safer than unsecured loans because, if the borrower defaults, the investor (or the mortgage pool management) has a claim on the property.

spread   the difference between asked and sales price of homes, expressed as a percentage. Example: Average homes were priced at $107,500 in the past year, and average sales prices were $102,300, a difference of $5,200. The spread is 4.8% ($5,200 ÷ $107,500).

straight-line depreciation   a method of computing depreciation in which the same amount is claimed each year throughout the useful life. Straight-line depreciation is required for real estate depreciation.

substitution   the tendency for lower-priced properties to sell before high-priced properties with the same or similar features; and for lower sales prices to affect the market value of the remaining comparable properties.

supply and demand   the driving forces of the real estate cycle, which includes three categories: financing, market, and rental. The supply of money determines interest rates, lender policies, and closing cost levels, as well as the willingness of lenders to work with real estate investors. The supply of housing and demand for new housing determines pricing of residential property as well as how long it takes for properties to sell, whether they sell at full price or at a discount (or premium), and whether or not bargains can be found under present conditions. The level of supply and demand for rentals determines market rates as well as vacancy levels and trends.

sweat equity   increases in property value resulting from time and effort on the part of the property owner. In the case of the fixer-upper, the more time and effort put in, the higher the profits from sweat equity.

tax deferral   any decisions made to avoid paying more taxes this year, by moving tax liabilities to future years.

tax planning   a form of financial planning with taxes in mind: timing of purchases and sales, offsetting capital gains and losses, and identifying tax benefits. Planning is also essential in order to identify deductibility limits, make appropriate depreciation elections, and identify the after-tax cash flow and profits from rental income investments.

turnover the number of times capital is reused to produce profits. The more frequently capital is turned over, the greater overall yield will be, assuming the desired profit margin is earned.

useful life an approximation of the number of years a capital asset can be depreciated, based on the class of asset.

volatility a measurement of market risk; the tendency for market value to changes gradually over time (low volatility) or to change erratically and unpredictably (high volatility).

yield the profit from investments, expressed as a yield. Annualized yield is expressed as the overall yield, adjusted as though the investment were held for exactly one year.

Index

Index

A

accelerated depreciation, 124
active participation, 120
adjusted gross income (AGI), 122
adjusted purchase and sales price,
   44–45
after-tax cash flow, 116–118
allocation, 19, 122, 160–162
American Society of Home Inspectors
   (ASHI), 14
amortization, 125
annualized yield, 87

B

balloon payment, 53
book value, 123
bridge loan, 52
Bureau of Labor Statistics
   (BLS), 149
buyer psychology, 81–83

C

capital improvements, 32
carry, 15
cash buyer, 116
cash flow:
   after-tax, 40, 116–118
   analysis, 93

budget, 103–104
calculations, 29
defined, 7–8
exceptional, 89
features, 14–15
fixer-upper, 87–88
guidelines, 107–111
negative, 50
positive, 31, 102–105
problems, 105–107
profits, 165–167
restrictions, 112–116
risks, 147, 155–156
worksheets, 40, 106, 110
competition, 69–70
compound return, 21
conformity, 67
construction and development REIT,
   158, 160
Consumer Price Index
   (CPI), 149
contingency, 57

D

debt service, 17
discount, 86
distressed properties, 49
diversification, 18, 153–160